Art as an Early Intervention Tool for Children with Autism

Howard /
COUNTY Library
6600 Cradlerock Way, Columbia, MD 21045

of related interest

Fun with Messy Play
Ideas and Activities for Children with Special Needs
Tracey Beckerleg
ISBN 978 1 84310 641 8

Playing, Laughing and Learning with Children on the Autism Spectrum
A Practical Resource of Play Ideas for Parents and Carers
2nd edition
Christy Gast and Jane Krug
Illustrated by Julia Moor
ISBN 978 1 84310 608 1

The Hidden World of Autism
Writing and Art by Children with High-functioning Autism
Rebecca Chilvers
Foreword by Uttom Chowdhury
ISBN 978 1 84310 451 3

The Girl Who Spoke with Pictures
Autism Through Art
Eileen Miller
Illustrated by Kim Miller
Foreword by Robert Nickel MD
ISBN 978 1 84310 889 4

Art as an Early Intervention Tool for Children with Autism

Nicole Martin

Jessica Kingsley Publishers
London and Philadelphia

First published in 2009
by Jessica Kingsley Publishers
116 Pentonville Road
London N1 9JB, UK
and
400 Market Street, Suite 400
Philadelphia, PA 19106, USA

www.jkp.com

Library of Congress Cataloging in Publication Data
A CIP catalog record for this book is available from the Library of Congress

British Library Cataloguing in Publication Data
A CIP catalogue record for this book is available from the British Library

ISBN 978 1 84905 807 0

Printed and bound in the United States by
Thomson-Shore, 7300 Joy Road, Dexter, MI 48130

This is for you, little brother.

With special love and thanks to my husband Daniel Jones, big hugs to everyone in my family, much gratitude for the support of my former colleagues and client families in Chicago, Illinois, and appreciation for the warm welcome I have received from my newly adopted home of Kansas.

Only through art can we get outside of ourselves and know another's view of the universe which is not the same as ours and see landscapes which would otherwise have remained unknown to us like the landscapes of the moon.

Marcel Proust

Much of the time, I feel like an anthropologist on Mars.

Temple Grandin

Contents

Why I Wrote this Book

Art as an Early Intervention Tool for Children with Autism is about making art with young kids on the spectrum—why it is important, how to go about it, and what to expect as you venture forth. It is written for both parents and professionals and designed to be accessible whatever your level of expertise. I know my audience is a busy one, so I have tried to keep the book short and sweet; in fact, there is a one-page summary of the book in Appendix B for those of you who may want to flip there now before diving into reading. And for those of you who want to dig deeper into the topic, the references and recommended reading lists will not let you down. Successful, therapeutic art-making with a child with autism is a very rewarding experience, and my goal is for you to feel well equipped but not overwhelmed. Please believe me: you do *not* have to be an artist to use the tools in this book.

My passion for this topic can be traced back to my own childhood experiences. In 1993 I was 11 years old and the eldest of four children. My youngest sibling, Jason, was three years old. My parents were worried that my brother might be deaf; I remember how hard it was to get Jason's attention, how oblivious he could seem to the activity around him. A few doctors' appointments and evaluations later, my family came to learn the meaning of a word that I had never heard before: autism.

As an 11-year-old girl, I dealt with this news in a way particular to my age and gender: I locked myself in my room and recorded it in my diary. Earlier entries had noted milestones such as "Jason said Mama today!" but soon those entries stopped and Jason lost his few words, retaining just a few vocalizations that only his family and teachers can decipher. It was not until Jason turned 16 that he began to say Mama again. I still get a lump in my throat even now as I write about it.

During my first year of high school I outgrew the diary and began making art, which I believe served the same purpose but provided me with a broader palette to express my teenage concerns. My brother and I had grown into very different people, but we also had our similarities. He would stare, fixated on his hands while I would "perseverate" in my own way, by making a series of artwork entirely about, well, hands. (I am now pretty good at drawing them.)

The same year that I learned about the field of art therapy and subsequently decided to become an art therapist was also the year that I began training to work as Jason's applied behavioral analysis (ABA) home therapist. Living in a small southwestern town, families like ours were few in number and in resources, and we had to become our own therapists and advocates. Applied behavioral analysis, as well as picture cards and sign language and everything else we tried, became a way of communicating with my brother, and consequently all my future clients, before I had even taken a single psychology course.

I would like to be able to say that I was the miraculous big sister, who saw the potential in her combination of skills in art and behavioral techniques, tailored programs to meet her brother's needs, and all around "saved" her brother from severe disability. The truth is I was an insecure adolescent, not brave enough to have any except the closest of friends visit my house lest my brother embarrass me, tuned like an antenna to the stresses and worries of my parents, and desperate to go to college and be on my own. When I think about the ways in which I would reinforce my brother's behaviors, like spinning objects or making what was affectionately coined "the scary face" (tensing his jaw and curling his fingers), I feel like I could laugh and cry at the same time. I was only trying to play with him; we as a family just didn't know any better. I was halfway through undergraduate school before I really started to grasp just how the arts could both address autism-related deficits and build on strengths. For me, art and autism are inextricably intertwined.

Needless to say, this work is very personal for me. Now that I am grown and a "real" therapist, there is a part of me that connects with each one of my clients, whether boy or girl, high or low functioning, that somehow goes beyond my training and touches deeply felt feelings for my brother and my family. I am absolutely aware that this is what therapists might describe as a "misplacement" of feelings about my brother onto a client, but that makes it sound negative, while I see it as a positive source of empathy. My family experience makes it automatic for me to draw from a reservoir of love and understanding for my clients. This is a skill for which I have my brother to thank.

Even when I received the necessary training, things were not always rosy. Being away from my family, not to mention working as a therapist yet unable to help out with my own brother, can be a real source of self-imposed guilt for a big sister. Also, I found that many professionals in the field of autism spectrum disorders had a minimal, or sometimes even erroneous, understanding of art therapy, even though they were often designing therapeutic arts programming of their own. Conversely, I could count on one hand the number of art therapists I knew who could name autism-specific interventions outside of our own field. This book is meant to act as a bridge toward mutual understanding between all people who make art with young children with autism—therapists, educators, parents, caregivers, and artists. I hope that it will inspire you toward further studies and new collaborations.

Art as an Early Intervention Tool for Children with Autism is about the relationship between art-making and young children with autism; it is an old idea put forth with a contemporary perspective. It is not a research book but rather a lovingly compiled description of the specialty told through the lens of my professional and personal experiences. Simply stated, art therapy and autism is about helping people on

The author and her brother a year before his diagnosis.

the spectrum utilize the visual arts to express and regulate themselves. Some individuals have a natural talent and are able to discover the benefits of making art on their own, but many more do not. What is liked or disliked, comfortable or uncomfortable, for people with autism is often determined very early in life. I believe that if therapeutic art-making was more often and more expertly integrated into early intervention treatment, we would see an improvement in these children's ability to tap into their imaginations.

This book is for you, busy moms and dads, interested therapists and teachers. Even if your child is past the age highlighted in this book, I think that you will still find most of the information very useful and applicable at any age. After an evening or two of reading you will understand a great deal about art and autism and be able to determine if this approach is right for your child.

1

Introduction to Autism Spectrum Disorders (ASD)

This chapter is designed to give readers who do not know much about autism a basic introduction to the disorder. A functional knowledge of autism is necessary in order to understand this book. Professionals working in the field or parents might consider skipping this chapter, but I would strongly encourage students, new professionals, and artists to read it carefully and check out the recommended websites listed at the end of the chapter.

What is autism?

Autism is defined by the current *Diagnostic and Statistical Manual of Mental Disorders* (American Psychiatric Association 2000) as a neurological disorder characterized by qualitative impairment in social interaction and communication as well as the presence of "restricted, repetitive, and stereotyped patterns of behaviors, interests, and activities" (American Psychiatric Association 2000, p.71). At present, we do not know what causes autism, therefore it is primarily described according to its signs and symptoms (how the person behaves). Traditionally, we think of autism in terms of what is referred to as the "triad of impairment": socialization, communication, and imagination. To greater or lesser degrees,

Children with autism truly represent a "spectrum" of talents, interests, and abilities.

these three problem areas have to manifest themselves in a person in order for them to receive a diagnosis of autism.

Socialization problems may present as disengagement, abruptness, lack of expressed empathy, or poor eye contact, among other things. Activities that we think of as making friends, remembering your manners, or maintaining relationships can be incredibly foreign to a child with autism. Socially based emotions like embarrassment or competitiveness often just do not exist. It can be difficult when a child prefers to be alone or does not seem particularly attached to other people, but children with autism do crave human affection and attention just like anyone else. Spend some time with them and you will see what I mean.

Difficulties with communication have to do with both the relative lack of it as well as common grammatical or syntax errors. Contextual questions (e.g., *why* did something happen) and pronoun use are common problem areas. Using figures of speech (e.g., "go jump in the lake") might be confusing for some children with autism, as they tend to be very literal, concrete thinkers. Difficulty expressing appropriate emotions can tangle up communication as well. The child's emotion may not match his or her message (e.g., laughing after sharing that the dog died) or if the child is experiencing strong emotions (such as frustration, sadness, desire, etc.) verbal communication may completely break down. A perceived halt in language development or even a loss of previously learned words is one classic indicator of autism, although, like other features, it does not necessarily apply to everyone. Many people with autism have large vocabularies and are primarily verbal communicators. Those who do not develop verbal language are often taught to communicate using visual languages, like exchanging picture cards or sign language. Overall, receptive language skills (understanding what is said) tend to be stronger than expressive language skills (speaking with clear communicative intent) for people with autism.

Imagination deficits can be a bit tricky to pinpoint, especially since, in my opinion, they are bound up with the child's need for a sense of order/control and sensory regulation. Symbolic play (or "pretend play") and creative activities (like art) require some exercise of the imagination, and rarely come naturally to a child with autism. Suppositions (e.g., what *would* you do?) can be very challenging, and the child will often search for a "correct" answer without understanding that there is no right or wrong when it comes to using your imagination. Difficulties with imagination may be related to a field of study called theory of mind, which is the ability to put yourself in another person's shoes, or imagine what they might be thinking. (Theory of mind is often considered to be a possible "fourth impairment" of autism.) What the *Diagnostic and Statistical Manual of Mental Disorders* (DSM) refers to as "restricted, repetitive, and stereotyped patterns of behaviors, interests, and activities" often present as a strict daily routine, getting very upset over minor interruptions in a favorite activity, a need to order the environment (even if it looks messy to us), and/or having a very short list of interests. Much of this inflexibility has to do with the person's need to regulate their sensory input. People with autism can be hyper (over) or hypo (under) stimulated by their environment, and it is often difficult to anticipate when or how this might happen. The sound of a crying baby or the jostle of a crowd, for example, can generate such strong anxiety in a child with autism that it makes perfect sense that they would try to circumscribe their daily activities as much as possible. Sensory needs can trump imaginative, exploratory (i.e., risky) endeavors. *Therapeutic art-making provides a variety of sensory stimulation in a safe, organized environment using activities that can crack open the door to a child's imagination.*

There are three terms that are important to be familiar with when working with people with autism: scripting, perseverating, and stimming. These are very common behaviors displayed by people with autism, mostly related to their sensory and control needs.

Scripting is a tendency to recite words or phrases that usually, but not always, originate from some outside source (e.g., quoting lines from a book or a T.V. show). Scripting is different from parroting, which is when a person repeats your words back to you (e.g., asking, "How are you?" and getting "How are you?" in response). Some people may use a script as a way to express themselves (e.g., saying "Hasta la vista, baby" from the Schwarzenegger movie instead of "I don't feel like working today"). Teaching the child an appropriate variety of "scripts" to use for different situations is often part of therapy.

Perseverating is an obsession with a topic. It does not have the word-for-word repetition of a script. A child might, for example, perseverate on baseball. It is good to have a passionate interest, but when you talk about baseball so much that it interferes with your ability to focus at school, it is a problem. Sometimes therapists or teachers refer to compulsive or repetitive behaviors (like turning a light switch on and off, or making only one stroke over and over with a paintbrush) as perseverating.

Stimming is shorthand for self-stimulating behaviors, which are odd behaviors that nevertheless satisfy the child's need for more, or different, sensory stimulation. Hand-flapping, spinning objects, hair-stroking, tongue-clicking, and so on are all "stims." Sometimes strong emotions, like frustration or excitement, can "overload" the sensory system and result in stimming. In some children stimming might manifest as inappropriate or self-injurious behaviors such as hair-pulling, public masturbation, or head-banging.

Since the characteristics and behaviors described above present to greater or lesser degrees in each individual, you can imagine the great variety of similarities and differences there can be among people with autism. Individuals with autism are often described by teachers and therapists as either "high functioning" (i.e., verbal, in mainstream classroom, etc.) or "low functioning" (i.e., nonverbal, severe sensory issues, etc.).

Disorders that are very similar to autism (technically called "autistic disorder") and yet retain their own different distinctions "on the spectrum" include childhood disintegrative disorder, pervasive developmental disorder not otherwise specified (PDD-NOS), Asperger's syndrome, and Rett's syndrome (see Table 1 for descriptions). To reflect this range, professionals now refer to autism as "autism spectrum disorder" (ASD). This book uses the terms "autism" and "autism spectrum disorder" (ASD) interchangeably since both are currently acceptable. Additional disorders such as seizure disorder, apraxia, fragile X syndrome, celiac disease, nonverbal learning disability, receptive and/or expressive language disorder, obsessive-compulsive disorder, attention deficit hyperactivity disorder, and dyslexia are sometimes considered to be part of an even broader continuum of ASD-like symptomology and therapists who work with children on the spectrum can usually treat these children as well. It is not uncommon for a child to have both a spectrum diagnosis and a diagnosis from this broader continuum.

It is important to note that autism is not the same thing as mental retardation (MR), although the majority of people with autism do have MR to some degree as well. MR is simply a classification for an individual whose IQ (often still measured using the Stanford-Binet or Wechsler) is below 70 points. Standardized testing is difficult to do with children on the spectrum due to their attention and communication deficits, so it is very possible that many children test lower than their actual level of intelligence. It is possible to have a diagnosis on the spectrum and have normal or even above average intelligence (usually more common with a diagnosis of Asperger's), although it is not terribly common. Individuals with more severe disability may always need

Table 1 Brief summary of ASD as described in the Diagnostic and Statistical Manual of Mental Disorders IV-TR (American Psychiatric Association 2000) and the International Classification of Diseases-10 *(World Health Organization 1992).*

Autism spectrum disorders (ASD) or autism

1. Autistic disorder (DSM), childhood autism (ICD)

    Social, communication, and imagination impairment plus restricted and repetitive behaviors (what most people think of when they use the word "autism").

2. Rett's syndrome

    Similar to 1. but present only in females (very unusual; all other disorders are mostly present in males), head growth deceleration, loss of skill using hands, and poor coordination.

3. Childhood disintegrative disorder

    Similar to 1. but clear regression after two or more years of normal development (children referred to as having "lost their words" or "retreating within themselves").

4. Asperger's syndrome

    Similar to 1. but no delay in language development or cognition (independent living is likely).

5. Pervasive developmental disorder not otherwise specified (PDD-NOS) (including atypical autism)

    Social and communication impairment and stereotyped behaviors present, but do not technically fit the full criteria for one of the categories above (often referred to as "high functioning" autism).

---

help with toileting and hygiene and may or may not be able to benefit from inclusive academic environments.

Savants (individuals who display an extraordinary and specific genius despite their autism which severely impairs other aspects of their lives) definitely get more media coverage than the average person with autism. While they are inspirational examples of the miracles and mysteries of the human brain, they are atypical (as rare as genius in the general population) and should not be thought of as an example of a typical person with autism.

So what is the most *likely* explanation for autism? Heredity. Scientists have been able to identify several genes that are close to, or in the neighborhood of, genes that will probably be implicated in autism. Also, it has been shown that identical twins, who share 100 percent of their genes, are much more likely both to have autism than are non-identical twins who only share about half of their genes. One thing is for sure, whether or not a person has autism is determined by a compli-cated mix of factors. There is compelling testimony that environmental factors such as food allergies, gastrointestinal problems, abnormal reac-tion to the thimerosal formerly present in the MMR (measles-mumps-rubella) vaccination, mercury build up in the body, trauma at birth, and a vulnerable immune system might play roles. In other words, just the right cocktail of genes in a person's genetic code combined with a triggering environmental factor or two might explain the origin of a person's autism. This nature *plus* nurture view is currently a popular way to explain a large variety of mental health problems, and we will have to wait and see whether or not it pans out as an explanation for autism. In the meantime, parents cannot wait for gene therapy, so they experiment with gluten-free diets, chelation therapy (to remove metals from the body), digestive hormone treatments, vitamins, neuroleptic drugs, hyperbaric chambers (oxygen therapy), and more, with the hope of alleviating even a fraction of their child's symptoms.

What does a child with autism look like? Usually, male. Three out of every four children with autism is a boy, which might implicate some role of the Y chromosome. Otherwise, there are no superficial fea-tures of autism, which can be both a blessing and a curse for families. Sometimes parents are thankful that their child looks no different from other children, but it can be uncomfortable when strangers attempt to interact with a child with the expectation that the child is typical. The fact that the child looks otherwise normal but can act so strange makes autism seem like a mysterious disability, especially when hyped as such by the popular press. When I was a little girl I had a lot of guilty feelings over wishing that my brother had Down's syndrome, because then our situation would be self-evident. And also because I figured a person with Down's would be able to interact with me *better* than my brother with autism, who could not really care less about playing with me most of the time. However sooner or later, the repetitive, or even injurious, behaviors of a person with autism will manifest as physical characteristics, whether from an unbalanced diet, lack of sleep, calluses and repetitive bruising, poor hygiene, anxiety, or medication side effects. One feature that you can't see easily is that the brains of children with autism are often a bit on the large side and have pervasive wiring differences (almost every major section of the brain is implicated) compared to a neurotypical person's brain.

According to recent statistics from the Centers for Disease Control and Prevention (2007), 1 child in 150 across 20 U.S. communities surveyed has a diagnosis on the spectrum. There is a lot of debate over such statistics (whether they show that numbers are on the rise or that professionals are better at giving accurate diagnoses), but what is important is that these children (and teenagers and adults) exist in higher numbers than expected and are in need of services.

Some people believe that a cure for autism will be found. And it is true that we have come a very long way since the 1960s when Bernard Rimland and other parents and researchers like him decided to take issue with the popular belief that autism was caused by poor parenting. Even the traditional age of onset (three years old) is being challenged. Cutting-edge therapists can diagnose symptoms as young as 14 months old now, which suggests that autism does not *happen* at age three but was lurking from birth, unnoticed to the untrained eye. In just the 18 years since my brother was born, advances in genetic research have made the possibility of a cure change from a pipe dream to being just out of reach. It will be interesting to see what the future holds.

As much as we love and accept the people we care for with ASD, I am sure that all families and therapists fantasize about what their child or student would be like without autism, and many would wish away that child's anxiety, awkwardness, and discomfort if they could. There is nothing I would love more than an early retirement because a cure for autism was found, but it will not be anytime soon. Good research takes time and, although these kids may be our number one priority, they are not necessarily the world's priority. Society doesn't funnel much public or private money toward social services in general, and autism is not the only disorder angling for a piece of that small pie. But it is encouraging to see how fast the information about autism has spread and seeped into the public consciousness these last few years. Loud and proud (and desperate) family members get most of the credit for this change.

No matter how much you learn about ASD in general, it is the specific person(s) with autism that you know who will act as your definition of what autism is. It cannot be helped. Obviously my definition was my brother until I became a therapist, and it took me a while to get used to the sheer variety of people who all qualify as being on the spectrum. And so for every description I have given of autism in this chapter, there will be exceptions. And for every generalization I have made, there are complex individuals living within the unique context of their lives, a much richer picture than I can paint in just an introductory chapter. In order to define autism, we list its differences and peculiarities, but it is what we share in common that connects us as people.

We all get songs stuck in our head (perseverating, scripting), have impractical but self-soothing rituals (need for order and routine), and can be unintentionally oblivious to others' feelings (unempathetic, asocial) but these behaviors don't consume us like they consume a person with autism. Like many disorders, autism spectrum disorders are certain aspects of human nature, magnified. Also, having ASD doesn't necessarily overshadow a child's natural talents, and building on these strengths rather than focusing strictly on tackling deficits is integral to successes in therapy. Children with autism hear "no" a lot from adults; helping them find ways to express and develop their talents lets them say yes to themselves.

2

Integrating Art into Early Intervention Treatment

Early intervention is the most dynamic and critical period in the treatment of children with autism for one very simple reason: the younger they are, the more "elastic" their brains are. At this age, neuronal connections are still being made in high quantity and are not yet set in stone. It is the window of time in which therapists and parents, by manipulating a child's environment and its demands upon the child, have the best chance of making changes in the wiring of the child's brain. "Early intervention," or "early childhood intervention," refers to the time frame between when a child is first diagnosed (at birth, for some disorders; for ASD, usually between 18 to 36 months old) and when they enter school (about age five). Early intervention treatment is usually a multidisciplinary approach, with a variety of therapists and teachers working in collaboration to improve the child's prognosis in every area of development. A child need only be old enough to manipulate materials to begin working on drawing (two to three years old is usually a good age to begin integrating art-making into therapy). This chapter answers a few specific questions about using art with children at this age; the rest of the book will round out all the necessary knowledge and strategies for carrying it out.

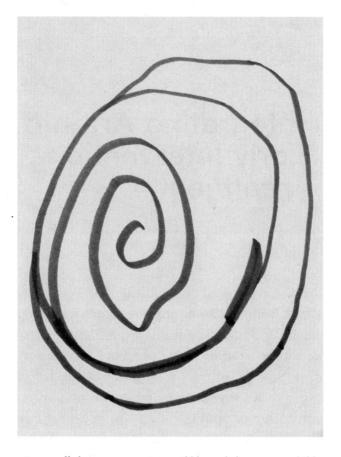

A controlled, age-appropriate scribble made by a young child with autism.

What it is about kids with autism that draws them to art

Art is an interesting crossroads for children with ASD because it is an activity in which strengths (visual learners, sensory interests) and deficits (imagination, need for sensory control) merge. They often desire art-making very much but then have a hard time engaging in it appropriately. (Children will often use art-making as an outlet for the symptoms that will be described in Chapter 3.) The general public seems to have the impression that children with autism making art is good, even magical, while simultaneously these children have a reputation for using art in an unusual or delayed manner. Meanwhile, traditional therapists often view art-making as either potentially regressive and perseverative, or at best as a good thing but with no clear therapeutic aim beyond technical skill-building. Despite this ambivalence they will still try to incorporate art into the child's therapeutic activities. Everyone appears to agree that art is beneficial to these children yet few people can articulate why this is or how to best go about it.

Most professionals who have studied children making art agree that art-making, that is, drawing, modeling, building, and so on, is a natural, inborn characteristic of all of us that begins as soon as we are old enough to grasp and manipulate tools. If you give a child a crayon, as long as it is no longer seen as food, she will scrawl with it until, over time, untaught, she will shape her scribbles into controlled, intentional drawings. There is no reason to assume that this ability is denied a child born with autism. Buried or impeded by symptoms like imagination deficits, anxiety and competing sensory distractions perhaps, but not denied. Also, some art theorists believe that not only is art-making innate, but it satisfies an innate aesthetic need in children. Again, there is no reason to assume this doesn't apply to kids with ASD as well; in fact, many demonstrate aesthetic preferences in their drawings. All in all, they are still kids and kids love art. In addition, art provides an outlet for their perseverative and self-stimulatory behaviors. I believe children with ASD are no more or less drawn to art than their neurotypical counterparts, but their symptoms can make it appear otherwise. For example, symptoms such as hyperfocus, a need for high detail, or a perseverative interest in colors are often interpreted as a "high" interest in art while tactile defensiveness or imagination deficits are used as indicators of "low" interest.

Art as rehabilitation

Very simply put, rehabilitation is a type of therapy that trains or exercises parts of the brain (or body) that have been impaired by disease or injury. Early intervention therapies for children with autism are re-habilitative therapies, working to manipulate weak or atypical connections in the brain. Autism is a pervasive "rewiring" of the brain, and creativity is also a complex, multi-lobe process. If the aim is to rehabilitate something as complicated as a child's creativity and imagination, what activity first springs to mind? Probably, the arts. Drawing is already used regularly for assessment (of imagination deficits, fine motor skills, visual-spatial deficits, developmental level, etc.), so it makes sense that art could be easily adapted for use as a practical therapy in this specialty.

Understanding the usefulness of art in early intervention treatment requires a few basic assumptions. First is that the adult is not fixing a child's artwork, but using art to "fix" parts of the child that can be *best* engaged using art. (I outline six major treatment goal areas in Chapter 4.) Next, the art itself (the product) is not as important as gaining the self-discovery, experimentation, tactile tolerance, and so on (the process) that is required to make it. The product becomes more important to the child (and useful to the therapist or teacher) as the child gets older, but when children are small the process is *much* more exhilarating to them than is admiring the finished piece. Third, we have to agree that skills such as imagination and creativity are worth rehabilitating in children with autism. With so many other pressing needs, like communication skills or toileting or sleeping through the night, less immediately practical training goals are sometimes neglected or put off until later unless the child shows an early interest or talent. This is very understandable, but it means losing precious time for helping *all* kids with ASD (not just the ones with early artistic talent) develop good art-making habits for a lifetime, which is easier to do while they are young. Last, you must believe that creativity *can* be learned. I know it is a hard knot to untangle and a little less clear-cut than other treatment goals, but it really is not any more complicated. Just because art-related skills such as experimentation and abstract thinking are usually able to develop in children without intervention, it does not mean that these skills are impossible to teach. A huge part of ASD therapies involves teaching equally abstract skills that we take for granted in neurotypical children, such as inferring unspoken parts of conversation, making value judgments and analyzing situations. Even neurotypical children do not learn in a vacuum; proper environmental stimulation appropriate to the child's needs is necessary for developing creative thinking in *all* children. Strategies for creating good learning environments for children on the spectrum are outlined in Chapter 6.

How to move past scribbling

The most common goal related to art that is addressed by well-meaning early intervention therapists involves helping a child with autism move from drawing "nothing" to drawing "something," that is, to move from scribbling into representational drawing. It is true that the early drawings of children on the spectrum can be very disorganized, compulsive, and perseverative and that there is a relationship between their ASD symptoms and their drawings (as I will outline in the next chapter). But non-art therapists or art educators often cannot or do not distinguish between "good" scribbling (focused, contemplative, experimental, sometimes even chaotic) and "bad" scribbling (symptomatic), both of which are present in children on the spectrum to greater or lesser degrees, and often try to skip past or minimize the child's age-appropriate period of scribbling.

A neurotypical child's early artistic development is really quite amazing. You can literally toss them a couple of crayons and a smile and leave the rest up to them. Pre-school age drawing is a period of self-teaching and experimentation that adults regularly take for granted. If you are making art with children on the spectrum, it is important to be familiar with the major theories of childhood artistic development and use this knowledge as your basis for comparison, as opposed to comparing the child's work to adult standards.

Two of the most influential theories in this field were developed by art educators Viktor Lowenfeld (1987) and Rhoda Kellogg (1969), both working in the United States (Lowenfeld in Pennsylvania, Kellogg in California) at the same time (from the 1940s to 1970s). Viktor Lowenfeld's extensive theory (published under joint authorship with W. Lambert Brittain) parallels the psychological needs of the child with the child's artistic growth from the toddler years to adulthood; his texts are still standards in the fields of both art education and art therapy. Lowenfeld described early childhood drawing as a progression from disorganized, random scribbling to more controlled scribbles, which the child will eventually begin to name, before entering the period of preschematic, conscious drawing with schemas/symbols that adults will recognize.

Rhoda Kellogg was a careful observer who collected and classified hundreds of thousands of drawings made by children from around the world. A slightly lesser known figure than Lowenfeld, Kellogg disagreed with the idea that scribbling is mainly a kinesthetic activity and believed that visual interest is essential (or else, why would the child bother?). She observed that children drew intuitively, without external models, according to their own, innate aesthetic sensibilities. Kellogg's documentation of the transition from scribbling to preschematic work (something that Lowenfeld's theory lacks) is very useful for understanding how to help a child move past scribbling, and illustrates the richness of this period (see Tables 2 and 3 for a summary).

Despite philosophical differences, both Kellogg and Lowenfeld agreed that scribbling is an important, innate, and exploratory activity influenced by the child's motor ability and physical growth. When it comes to children on the spectrum (and all children for that matter), I would add sensory discomfort/distraction and unique aesthetic vision as additional influencing factors. Of course any developmental theory, created with average children (neither autistic nor talented) in mind, should be taken with a grain of salt. Both Lowenfeld and Kellogg formed their ideas with the assumption that children freely roam in and learn from their environment, that they seek out novelty, and that they are not being constantly bombarded by uncomfortable sensory stimuli.

Table 2 Viktor Lowenfeld's early childhood artistic development theory as simplified by the author.

VICTOR LOWENFELD

Text: *Creative and Mental Growth* (Lowenfeld 1947, 1952, 1957, 1964, 1970, 1975, 1982, 1987)

Scribbling stage (18 months to 4 years):
Described as a time of kinesthetic pleasure and developing one's attitude toward art-making.

(1) Disorganized scribbling: No control; random marks.

(2) Controlled scribbling: Increasing variety and experimentation.

 = Daddy

(3) Named scribbling: Little change in the drawing itself, but giving it a name, thus thinking of it in representational terms.

Preschematic stage (4–7 years):
Described as the beginning of conscious art-making. All art is believed to be a direct reflection of the child's life and interests ("egocentrism"). Basic schemas/symbols are developed; first is that of a "man."

Table 3 Rhoda Kellogg's early childhood artistic development theory as simplified by the author.

RHODA KELLOGG

Text: *Analyzing Children's Art* (Kellogg 1969)

From approximately 18 months to 4–5 years of age:
A progression of foundational skills...

Basic scribbles (such as dot, line, closed loop, etc.): Can be made intentionally or accidentally.

Placement patterns: The deliberate decision of where to place a mark on the paper.

Emergent diagram shapes: Honing scribbles into shape.

Diagrams: What we conventionally call "shapes" such as triangle and cross.

Combines: Two diagrams together.

Aggregates: Three or more diagrams together.

...which are then utilized to create first schemas.

First, mandalas: Then, suns:

Next, radials:

Last, humans:

From 4–7 years, there is increasing variety and schema development, including animals, buildings, trees, flowers, and transportation vehicles.

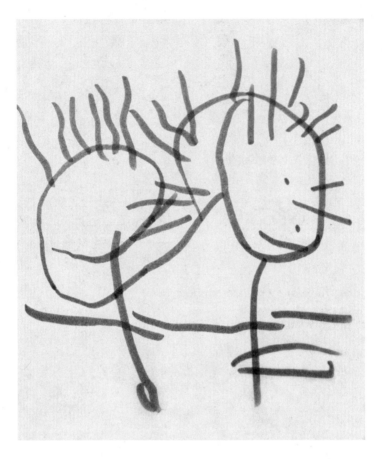

"Sun people" drawn by a three-year-old child on the spectrum after intervention. Described in Rhoda Kellogg's book and very age-appropriate!

In the next chapter, I outline several common characteristics of the artwork of children on the spectrum that diverge from the norm, first and foremost being atypical or delayed artistic development, such as being "stuck" at the scribbling stage, fluctuating between scribbling and schematic work, or skipping over the scribbling stage entirely. If a child with ASD is stalled out at the scribbling level (at any age) and you believe he can do better, there are several things you can do to help him move on:

Healthy scribbling: A nice, healthy aggregate drawn by a usually perseverative three-year-old scribbler.

Look for healthy scribbling and encourage it

What is healthy scribbling? That which involves experimentation, flexibility, and variety. Train yourself to look for and identify scribbles of the kind that Kellogg recorded (see Table 3) and keep the developmental path that she describes in mind as your goal. When you see healthy scribbles, reinforce the child's good work.

Evaluate environmental conditions

Help the child focus by reducing extraneous sensory stimuli (sights, sounds, smells, etc.) and/or by organizing the room to make expectations clear and maximize comfort. Provide the structure and predictability that children on the spectrum so often crave but change projects or work stations often enough to discourage too much rigidity. The goal should be for the child to eventually be able to make art in a natural environment, such as at home or school.

Provide visual supports

Children with autism are often highly visual (enjoy visual stimulation, need visual instructions to improve comprehension, some even have photographic memories) and giving a little visual "nudge" can help a lot:

- *Visual starters* (e.g., drawing a horizon line or a circle) prompt the child to "complete" the drawing, and are a bit like an artist making a big swipe across the canvas so that it is no longer blank and daunting.

- *Visual models* can be anything the child references to help inspire drawing (a toy, a picture, a drawing by an adult).

- *Visual instructions* can be in pictorial and/or written format and provide clear structure and expectations. Make sure that these are simplified as the child will probably be distracted by extraneous information in the images.

Modify tasks into manageable parts

If needed, break projects down into their smallest parts. For example, "draw a house" actually means draw two horizontal lines and two vertical lines (a box or square), then two lines that come to a point on top (making a triangle), and so on.

Provide physical, sensory support

Read Chapter 6 for ways to help children regulate their bodies, and provide this support as needed. Regulating their bodies usually improves the quality of their artwork considerably. (*Rule of thumb: Directly impact the child's symptoms to indirectly impact the child's artwork.*) If the child is using art materials in an inappropriate self-stimulatory way, provide them with a substitute (e.g., if chewing on a paintbrush, provide something appropriate to chew). Some scribblers will start off okay but then get carried away by the kinesthetic feeling of making the strokes. Providing gentle pressure on the wrist or shoulder, paired with a verbal or visual prompt to "slow down", can help. Hand-over-hand prompting can be good practice but fade out the pressure of your own hand as soon as possible. This can be used more to educate the child on how their body should feel and move to complete the task, rather than as a way to do the task itself.

Don't discourage independent work, no matter what

Amend, modify, or slow down perhaps, but never discourage a child's independent artwork. Celebrate drawings, even if you know they are less than the child's best, but give those best drawings an extra special reinforcement. Nurture and shape where the child is at, and do not give them things out of left field to copy. Topic ideas should come from the child as much as possible and from the adult as little as possible. Keep things neutral when the child's work is less than their best.

Name and isolate scribbles

Not only is it fun but naming scribbles helps the child visually isolate one mark from the next, practice abstract thinking, and paves the way for preschematic drawing. Encourage the child to come up with personalized names for their basic scribbles (e.g., vertical lines are "railroad tracks" or "tiger stripes," dots are "popcorn," "eyeballs," "ants," etc.). Other fun ways to help the child to distinguish between different marks/scribbles include pairing a mark/stroke with a sound, song, picture, character, story, or any prompt. Divide up your page like a grid to keep the scribbles separate and clear.

Have fun

Someone once said, "play is a child's work" but for a child with autism, appropriate play is *hard* work. Remember to be enthusiastic and keep

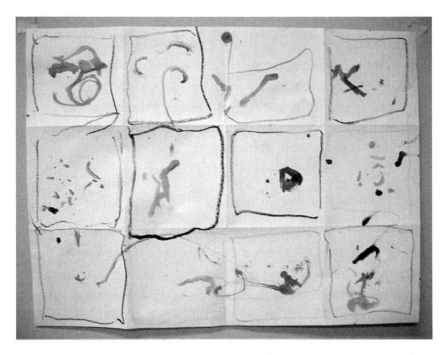

Help the child visually isolate and identify their many different kinds of scribbles. You are working to "tease out" one mark from the rest and help the child become a more organized and deliberate scribbler.

things light, clown around, coach them on. Sing your instructions, give their "drawing hand" a tickle or warm-up massage, take breaks for necessary things like snack and potty break. Try to create a fluid relationship between demands and rewards (so that it all, as much as possible, seems like fun) and do not fight their perseverative or otherwise symptomatic artwork when it arises. Shape it through reinforcement and compromise with the child, but make it a point of tension or interest and the child is sure to keep doing it.

Express your faith and confidence in the child's abilities

As young artists with autism gain more skill and control and progress toward preschematic drawing, they may become frustrated with their work. Ironically, as a child with ASD becomes more invested in art-making, he will sometimes hold himself to a higher standard of skill or detail than is age-appropriate (even as young as ages three to five). Young artists with autism are often more self-critical than their neurotypical peers. Help the child make comparisons, when appropriate or helpful, between his work and that of his peers (and not adults) and help him to see the glass as half-full instead of half-empty. Build up the child's self-confidence and help him develop a healthy attitude toward drawing. Do not let the child give up on a goal out of frustration; anything can be broken down into its smallest parts and learned.

Make art too

Don't just help the child, make art too. Work side-by-side or together with the child; you are acting as a live model. Give children a turn in the driver's seat; copy or imitate *their* best work to get their attention, praise them, and create a two-way flow of learning; even let them give you instructions. Make sure that you draw with them at their skill level or at the skill level you are working toward, rather than at an adult or professional level. This is most important if the child is young and/or learning how to draw. (A higher skill level often fascinates and frustrates a young artist with autism.) Demonstrate the age-appropriate process of discovery, exploration, and healthy scribbling for the child. (Therapists call this "modelling.")

Maintain the gain

The strength of their symptoms can be rather cyclical, which means children with ASD can fluctuate a bit in their drawing level from week to week. Make sure that the child has truly mastered a particular drawing or scribble by practicing it and monitoring to see if the child can draw it independently across a span of at least three or four consecutive sessions (a behaviorist rule of thumb).

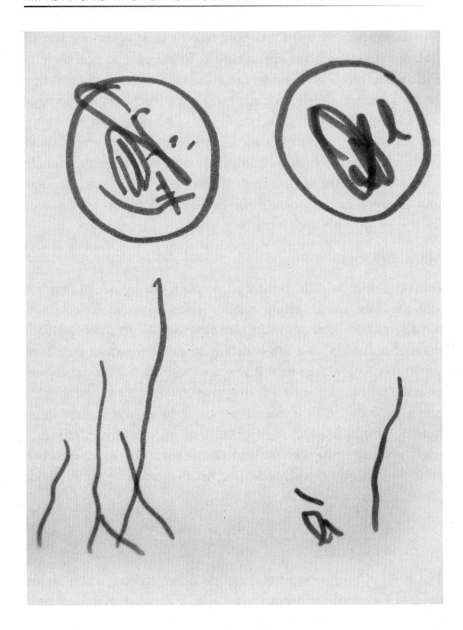

Visual starters: This child was beginning to name her scribbles, but still drawing in a disorganized and highly kinesthetic fashion. I drew two circles to give her a point of reference for her named scribbles (facial features inside the circles, the little marks below are " feet"). Just a week or two later she was making drawings like the one on the right. (I still had not drawn any models for her other than the circle!)

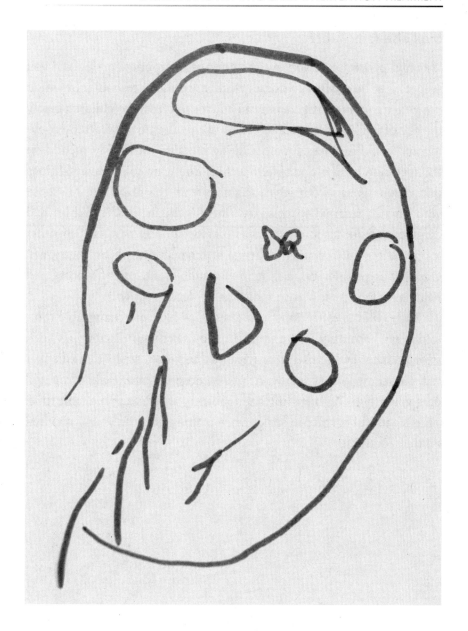

Visual model: This child mostly drew simple, perseverative scribbles (like the "perseverative puddles" described in the next chapter) but showed an interest in a little fireman toy. Without verbal instructions I drew a picture of it, pointed to it, and left it on her table. She drew the aggregate scribble on the right while referencing my drawing. An age-appropriate scribble that demonstrates attention to detail—fantastic!

If all else fails, teach

If a child persists in scribbling past the age-appropriate period and you suspect that he or she can do better, then try direct teaching. Imitation drawing ("copying") is generally a bad idea to present to children below the age of five. Neurotypical children of this age do not learn by copying and could care less about imitating models. (Obviously, a child on the spectrum cares even less about this.) You want to create conditions that encourage drawings that originate from the child, but for those who do not respond to this, try teaching them basic scribbles and diagrams before teaching schemas (person, house, tree, etc.) in order to give the child a chance to arrive at schematic work on their own. Copying is popular because it is measurable and often "works," but being able to copy is a poor indicator of creative growth.

Each child is different, so use these tips like interchangeable tools to pull out according to the situation and use at your discretion. Quick reinforcement and praise, improvisation, and enthusiasm are skills that will also come in very handy. As a keen observer and teacher, you will paradoxically be both leading and following the child at the same time. This is a useful balance to strike when making art with young children on the spectrum.

3

Characteristics of Artwork Made by Children with Autism

There is a unique beauty and style to the art made by people with autism. Children on the spectrum experience the world and their bodies differently than their neurotypical peers, and their artwork reflects this difference. There are several observable characteristics that are remarkable enough to warrant description as an autism-related style of art-making. Just like the general symptoms of an ASD diagnosis, at least a few of these art characteristics are present to greater or lesser degrees in each young artist with autism, and the characteristics encompass a wide variety of children. In reality it is possible for *any* child's art-making to present one of these features at some point in time, but it is the pervasive nature of these characteristics and the way that they appear to stall out a typical artistic development that make them uniquely autistic features.

Matching the symptom to the style

This chapter is organized by clustering artwork characteristics with the most likely related ASD symptom. Keep in mind that ASD behaviors are interconnected, and a single characteristic may spring from more than one symptom. For example, "perseveration puddles" are most likely due to both perseveration and self-stimulatory behaviors, perhaps even

A young artist adding rainbow details to a self-portrait.

imagination deficits. To avoid repetition (and confusion), I picked the most likely symptom and stuck with it. The categories in and of themselves are not terribly important; what is more important is that they help us better understand the relationship between the symptoms of autism and the children's art-making processes so that we can design better interventions and environments for them.

Unless otherwise noted, the terminology used to describe artwork characteristics is my own invention and does not comprise terms that therapists in the field would necessarily recognize. I encourage adults to refrain from using these or any definitions to describe a child's art unless the child's behavior was observed while they made the artwork.

ASD symptom 1: Atypical or delayed development in one or more areas (speech/communication, imagination, social, etc.).

ARTWORK CHARACTERISTICS

Artistic developmental delay. The developmental level of a child with ASD as indicated by their drawings is related to the child's non-verbal mental age, which is often but not always delayed, according to researchers Tony Charman and Simon Baron-Cohen (1993). Delayed development means that the child is meeting the same milestones in the same order as a typical child but at a later age or slower pace. My own study (Martin 2008) showed that drawing can indicate a child's developmental level but not necessarily their specific diagnosis, and corroborated Charman and Baron-Cohen's claim that exceptional or even age-appropriate drawing skill is not a widespread feature of autism. Examples might include delayed onset of drawing or an artistic development stalled out at the scribbling stage.

Atypical artistic development. Atypical development means that a child's growth is not following the typical trajectory and might have unusual or out-of-order features. A few characteristics that have been noticed in children with ASD include skipping the preschematic stage of drawing (moving from unintelligible scribbles to recognizable figures with little or no experimental stage inbetween), unconventional choice of subjects (Selfe 1983), or precocious drawing ability.

ASD symptom 2: Need for completion

ARTWORK CHARACTERISTICS

Stacking. Stacking is mostly seen in clay work. It involves lumping all of the parts together with more concern for their presence than their placement, for example, piling "head," "body," "arms," "legs" on top of each other to create a figure rather than a coherent, if not correct, placement.

Cramming. This is mostly seen in drawings and paintings. Cramming is similar to stacking in the importance it places on

Cramming: This artist began drawing without planning ahead to allow for legs and so tacked them on at the end. She was much more interested in accomplishing the face and hand details.

completion rather than composition. The child will often begin drawings with little attention to placement and then run out of room on the paper and "cram" in the remaining features.

Impulsive correction/completion. This is described as a low threshold of tolerance for any perceived omission on a drawing or the impulse to self-correct or to make corrections (with or without permission) on others' drawings. Stacking, cramming, and impulsive correction/completion are not unusual behaviors for neurotypical (non-autistic) children, but for children with ASD they seem to persist past a developmentally appropriate age and might also be related to obsessive-compulsive feelings or visual-spatial deficits.

High detail. The tendency to include an unusually high amount of detail in his or her drawings is typically first noticed once a child is drawing at the preschematic level. Children who draw in this manner appear unable to filter out extraneous detail and compulsively include it in their artwork; these children usually develop reputations as artists. This behavior is often described as hyperfocus or "high fidelity attention" (Rimland 1978) in artistic savants. The need for high detail may be related to perceptual/sensory issues, perseveration and obsessive-compulsive behavior, or the need for order and organization, particularly if it involves drawing maps or floor plans.

ASD symptom 3: Need for order and organization

ARTWORK CHARACTERISTICS

Color sequencing. This is the one characteristic that adults seem to notice and comment on to me most often. Color sequencing is described as the need to use color in a rigid order. It is often expressed through use of the rainbow schema according to the ROYGBIV (red-orange-yellow-green-blue-indigo-violet) palette, although I have seen children given a randomly organized color palette follow its non-ROYGBIV order just as rigidly. Color sequencing is usually seen in drawing and painting—the work is often non-representational, just a stroke or blob will satisfy the child—but can also occur with colored clays.

Color labeling. This involves labeling something (a person, building, event, etc.) a particular color (e.g., "Monday is red"). The reason for the particular color choice can be hard to determine.

Cataloging. Cataloging is usually seen in drawing. It involves creating a visual catalog of interests, often with some relationship to

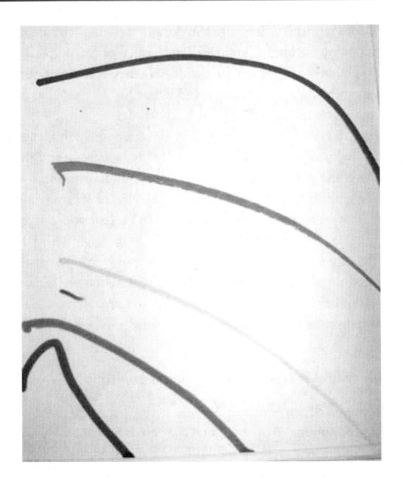

Color sequencing: Rainbows are popular subjects for many children (usually because taught to them by adults) but kids with ASD are often powerfully and naturally drawn to them due to their rigid and predictable color order.

each other (e.g., drawing different models of trains, different species of beetles, etc.). "Cataloging" is a frequently used term (not my own) to describe artwork by artists with ASD. Characteristics in the order and organization category seem to be related to perseveration and are often very self-soothing and satisfying to perform.

ASD symptom 4: Imagination deficits or concrete/literal thinking

ARTWORK CHARACTERISTICS

Difficulty with subject development. It can be difficult for kids with ASD to come up with their own ideas (beyond their current perseverative interest, if there is one) and they will often look to you or the environment for what seems like clues to the "right" answer. Working to help a child develop this skill requires a lot of patience, but it is one of the most important art-related goals to pursue.

Self-portrait features imposed on others. I suspect this is also related to the need for completion, schema stalemate (a self-portrait is often used as the child's basic human schema), pronoun difficulties, perhaps even theory of mind. I have watched kids draw me with

Self-portrait features imposed on others: A portrait of the author with two big pimples. I checked in the mirror afterwards and (I swear) those pimples were not there but the person who drew it was currently preoccupied with her own pimples. Can also see high pressure/perseverative strokes and need for detail.

glasses, freckles, pimples, hair color, and more that I do not have (but they did).

Lack of experimentation. Neurotypical children experiment quite a bit with drawing designs and schemas and often seek out new and unfamiliar sensory experiences; this hands-on experimentation behavior is often lacking in children with ASD. It is most likely related to sensory issues and atypical development.

Difficulty with non-veridical representations. "Non-veridical" means "not real". This characteristic is described in a study by Craig, Baron-Cohen, and Scott (2001) that used a variety of imaginative drawing tasks to isolate an autism-specific imagination deficit. Drawing something that does not exist in reality is a challenge for many kids on the spectrum.

ASD symptom 5: Perseveration or obsessive-compulsive type behaviors

ARTWORK CHARACTERISTICS

Graphic perseveration. Graphic perseveration refers to a persistent theme or topic in the child's artwork (e.g., a particular TV show character, cars, horses, rainbows, etc.). Having a favorite subject to draw is common in children (and adults for that matter) but for a child with ASD it is often at the expense of having other interests. A graphic perseveration differs from a favorite schema or a thematic body of artwork due to the child's inflexible and compulsive behavior. Graphic perseverations are often a big part of why a certain child "loves art" because it operates as a vehicle for the child's perseverative behavior and can be either a powerful help or hindrance in an art-making session, depending upon how it is managed by the adult. Graphic perseveration might be related to imagination deficits or the need for order and organization.

Schema stalemate. A schema stalemate is when the development of the child's schemas stalls out. Once the child has determined how to

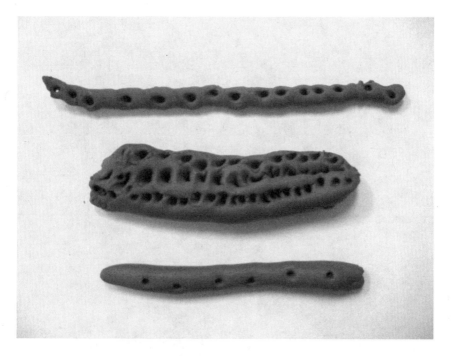

Graphic perseveration: Making "flutes" to express the perseverative enjoyment of poking holes.

draw "person," "house," and so on, minimal if any changes are made to these schemas without intervention. The child seems comfortable with their schemas and has little motivation or desire to change them despite the opinions of others. This is possibly related to lack of experimentation or social deficits.

Perseveration puddles. Perseveration puddles are a commonly seen product and are described as the kinesthetic and sensory enjoyment of dumping paint onto paper, even when that child has the ability to work at a representational level. Sometimes it involves placing each puddle of paint in a systematic way, one color at a time, like color sequencing. All behaviors in the perseveration/obsessive-compulsive category appear to reduce anxiety for many children with ASD so be sure to compromise with them about how and when these behaviors are okay while also helping them to become more flexible.

Perseveration puddles: Carefully, lovingly placed blobs of paint.

ASD symptom 6: Visual-spatial deficits

ARTWORK CHARACTERISTICS

Difficulty with sculpture. It is not uncommon for the modeling skills of a child with ASD to lag behind their drawing skills, and this will affect their preferences. Two-dimensional work (drawing or painting on a flat plane) is usually easier to manage and thus more desirable than three-dimensional work (building or modeling "in the round", i.e., from several angles/vantage points). Even drawings will often retain a flattened-out look beyond a developmentally appropriate age. Difficulty with sculpture is probably related to delayed development and tactile defensiveness.

ASD symptom 7: Sensory issues

ARTWORK CHARACTERISTICS

Use of materials for self-stimulation. Many children with autism seek stimulation constantly with whatever is within reach, so it is no surprise that they would do this with art materials too. Behaviors include mouthing, rolling, spinning, dropping, splashing, picking, smearing, smelling, pressing, and more. Providing appropriate substitutions (massage, a drink, a bean bag to squeeze, etc.) or teaching the child appropriate art tasks that involve some of these behaviors is helpful.

Tactile defensiveness. This term (not my own) is used a lot by autism therapists. Tactile defensiveness is a sensitivity to touch, and might include pressure, temperature, or textures. Children with ASD can be easily hyperstimulated, and touching wet, slippery, or crumbly materials is sometimes hard for them to tolerate. Dried clay or paint on the hands can be uncomfortable.

Art materials' impact on regulation. In my experience young children with autism usually gravitate toward art materials that roughly match or exacerbate their current sensory state (e.g., wanting thick, sloppy paints when already overstimulated). Training can help them learn to use art materials that help soothe and regulate (see Chapter 4 for more).

ASD symptom 8: Cyclical nature of ASD symptoms

ARTWORK CHARACTERISTIC

Artistic developmental level fluctuation. The intensity of some ASD symptoms appears to be cyclical for many children, with some days or weeks being better than others. Also, illness or a change in routine can exacerbate behaviors. On days like these a child's drawing level will often regress and the artwork characteristics listed in this chapter will become more pronounced. Because of this fluctuation, observing at least several drawings and art sessions is necessary before making any kind of assessment or conclusion about the child's drawing skill or ability.

ASD symptom 9: Social deficits

ARTWORK CHARACTERISTICS

Lack of insecurity about drawing ability. Children with autism do not seem to compare their drawings to the drawings of other children and judge their ability. Nor do they independently compare their own past and present drawings to reflect on their progress without adult prompting. Any critical attitudes that a child might have toward their artwork (that I have witnessed) usually seem related to need for completion or need for order and organization.

Lack of social learning or seeking models. Observing and spontaneously imitating the actions of others is a common deficit area for children with autism. Art groups and joint tasks can be very laborious for both the adults, who have to facilitate and prompt most of the social interaction at first, and the children, who have a great deal of social discomfort and sensitivities to noise, space, and touch. But the improvement in the child's social skills makes it more than worth the effort.

So what about the children's general attitude toward art-making? Just like neurotypical kids, most young children with ASD are highly interested in art materials. But this interest can fade as the child's primary interests (T.V., computer, etc.) become more circumscribed without intervention. Also, art-making might be stressful to the child because it feels like adults become punitive. This can occur when the child is unable to follow along during school projects, or senses parent/teacher anxiety over making messes spirals into a hyperstimulated state without

Table 4 Summary of Chapter 3.

ASD symptom	Artwork characteristics
1. Atypical or delayed development	Artistic developmental delay Atypical artistic development
2. Need for completion	Stacking Cramming Impulsive correction/completion High detail
3. Need for order and organization	Color sequencing Color labeling Cataloging
4. Imagination deficits/concrete or literal thinking	Difficulty with subject development Self-portrait features imposed on others Lack of experimentation Difficulty with non-veridical representations
5. Perseveration or obsessive-compulsive type behaviors	Graphic perseveration Schema stalemate Perseveration puddles
6. Visual-spatial deficits	Difficulty with sculpture
7. Sensory issues	Use of materials for self-stimulation Tactile defensiveness Art materials' impact on regulation
8. Cyclical nature of ASD symptoms	Artistic developmental level fluctuation
9. Social deficits	Lack of insecurity about drawing ability Lack of social learning or seeking models

proper adaptations or structure. An environment that is nurturing to a neurotypical child's creative development (lots of freedom, variety of materials easily on hand) can feel punishing to a child with autism who usually needs structure and predictability, and often feels overwhelmed by choices. An adult should take all these factors into consideration before deciding that a child does or does not like art.

Is this chapter a list of "bad" things that children with ASD do that we should try to "fix"? Absolutely not. These are descriptions, not value judgments. Just because the artwork characteristics described in this chapter are associated with autism does not mean that they should be avoided or looked upon badly. I also do not believe that artwork by children with autism should be protected as "pure expression" and large deficit areas left unaddressed. Free (i.e., unsupported) art expression is never more important than the child's quality of life. Some characteristics, like color labeling, cataloging, and high detail, can result in some very cool artwork while others, like use of materials for self-stimulation and difficulty with sculpture, should be dealt with as behaviors to change or improve. We need to help children learn how to use art in a way that is life-enhancing; there are many ways that young kids with ASD naturally use art materials that are *not* life-enhancing. Compromise with the child and create interventions that complement the child's natural tendencies while helping them to express themselves beyond their symptoms.

Artistic/autistic?: Let's talk about artist savants

Even before I knew much about the nature of autism, I knew that people with autism could make art. The psychologist Bernard Rimland was for my family, as for many others, a kind of hero figure and my mother used to buy greeting cards that featured paintings by Dr. Rimland's son, Mark, a well-known artist with autism. Although this book is designed to address the needs of *most* young children on the spectrum (and savants are a minority), the talents of artist savants are related to the drawing characteristics outlined in this chapter, and besides, it is a relevant topic I cannot afford to ignore. So let's talk about it.

A savant is simply defined as a person whose extraordinary skill in one area stands out in sharp contrast to their other, much lower-functioning skills (e.g., someone who can play Beethoven's *Fifth Symphony* flawlessly after only hearing it once but still cannot bathe independently). Usually the disability is autism, mental retardation, blindness, or schizophrenia and if the person wasn't disabled, he or she would just be called a "genius." As Darold Treffert (1989) says in his book *Extraordinary People*, not all people with autism are savants, and not all savants have autism. Autism is rare, savant skill within autism is rare, and among the common talent areas (including calendar calculation, musical ability, memorization, etc.), art-making is rare. So an artist savant on the spectrum is a truly exceptional person.

Treffert describes two types of savants: talented savants and prodigious savants. Talented savants are more common and can often be found as adults working in accessible artist studios and exhibiting their artwork. A prodigious savant is a person with a jaw-dropping talent that is unusual for *anyone*, like for example, artist Steven Wiltshire making a detailed aerial view drawing of Rome from memory—down to the number of columns on St. Peter's—after one helicopter ride.

People debate whether savant skills are *in spite of* disability or *because of* disability; that is, whether the brain is composed of "islands of intelligence" which allow music or art skills to function independently of general intelligence, or if features of the disability (e.g., limited range of interests, hypersensitivity, etc.) create conditions that funnel any ability of the child down into one very narrow skills set. In the case of a savant with autism, the characteristics of ASD itself (such as perseveration or obsessive-compulsive type features, need for organization, high fidelity focus, or "thinking in pictures" to quote Temple Grandin) seem magnified, intensified, or channeled into a productive activity.

Artist savant skills are related to impressive visual memory and technical skill, and are not automatic indicators of creativity, abstract thinking, or emotional expression. Just like their non-savant peers with autism, imagination, emotions, and self-expression are deficit areas for savants, and good technical drawing or sculpting ability does not change this. This is all the more reason why I think copying activities are a less than ideal way to introduce a young child to art. People who draw well are not necessarily imaginative and people who are imaginative do not always draw well. This book describes six treatment goals in the next chapter that are ideal to address using therapeutic art tasks. But would they still be a good idea if the child had savant art skills? That is, would an artist savant in art therapy be a good idea or a bad idea? I am sure that those of you who know a child on the spectrum with artistic talent are wondering whether or not they would "need" art therapy (since they are already so good at drawing) or worry that intervention might upset some fine balance and cause the child to lose his or her talent—truly a very precious thing.

Worries like this are understandable but unjustified. The goal of art therapy is not to try to turn a child who isn't particularly good at drawing into Picasso and it is not to "correct" the quirky drawing style of a person with autism either. Art therapy is a supportive environment that encourages the child's interests and uses them to engage the child in working on deficit areas. This is essentially a "teaching to the child's strengths" approach, which, from this framework, would mean that art therapy with artist savants has great potential.

The approach described in this book encourages behavioral interventions, which derives from my experience working with applied behavioral analysis (ABA) specialists. Some people are suspicious of interventions that seem to be (or might have been in the past) in conflict with encouraging creativity. But I believe that blending in some behavioral techniques into art-making is very useful; trying to redirect a child to use art when they are having a meltdown without some kind of behavioral finesse is not going to work.

Anyone worried about behavior management or symptom reduction ruining a savant's talent are usually thinking of the famous case of Nadia, a young artist savant who over the course of therapy, family tragedies, and simply aging, lost her extraordinary drawing skill (Henley 1989). There are many cases to the contrary of artist savants who were able to improve their overall functioning and behaviors without any tarnishing of their talent. The case of Nadia often just stirs up myths of incompatibility between art-making and behavioral therapies. In my experience, behavioral interventions *improve* the quality of the child's artwork and, conversely, making art can sometimes improve behaviors.

In the art world, unusual is good. Artwork made by artist savants with autism, often described as "methodic", "quirky", "intense," or "primitive," is in high demand in the "outsider" art market (the term "outsider" refers to art made by non-professionals often with little or no formal training, sometimes with neurodevelopmental disabilities or mental illness). The freshness and lack of self-consciousness of these works is very appealing. I think that the artwork of a person with autism is uniquely beautiful mostly because they do not care what you think about them or their artwork; an artist savant, because of her autism, is often too rigid to learn from others and is left alone to develop her own personal aesthetic (and her art is probably the closest thing to Rhoda Kellogg's ideal of letting a child's art develop without adult correction as is possible). It's hard to separate an artist from her art, and the style of the artist savant's work (whether highly detailed, cataloging, etc.) is inherently bound up with the symptoms of her autism, and the work is better for it. It is possible to tackle the six deficit areas outlined in the next chapter while preserving the unique drawing style of a child, savant or not.

4

Why Art Projects Are Beneficial

The power of art for kids with autism lies in its ability to make learning both visual and appealing. The promise of fun art projects will often grab and hold the child's interest while the adult can ensure that the projects are designed to help the child make progress in relevant treatment goal areas. I believe that there are six major goals for children on the spectrum that can be best addressed using art:

1. imagination/abstract thinking

2. sensory regulation and integration

3. emotions/self-expression

4. developmental growth

5. visual-spatial skills

6. recreation/leisure skills.

All children on the spectrum will have deficits in at least one of these areas. As you read the chapter, think about which goal(s) best describe your child's needs. I have organized the chapter by pairing *goals* (the deficit area or long-term goal to target) with *specialied art projects* designed to address the long-term goal. I only list a few of my favorite

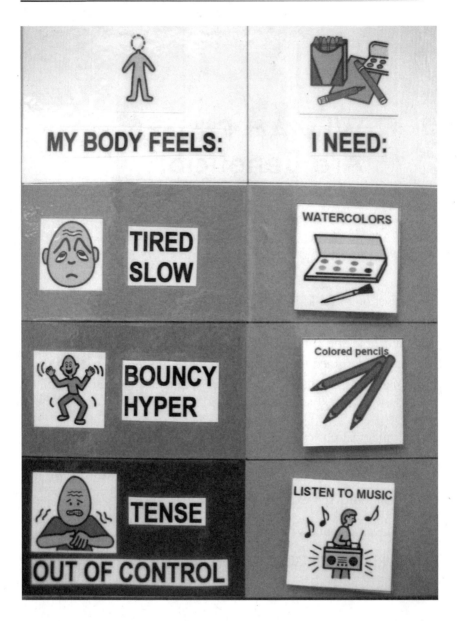

A visual aide created to help a child learn how to self-regulate using art.

projects; there are numerous other possibilities, and creating new projects with a specific child in mind is really the best way to work.

Some of the projects I list are for school-age children and will be too difficult for children in the early intervention age range; the needs for children under the age of five will mostly cluster in the sensory regulation and integration category. However, it will be helpful to know what you are working toward and to see the big picture. Also, some goals and projects will be more appropriate than others depending on where the child falls on the spectrum (their "level of functioning"). The next chapter, Tools of the Trade, describes the art materials themselves and is the sister to this chapter.

1. Imagination/abstract thinking

Goal

To display age-appropriate imagination and abstract thinking skills.

Imagination, to a greater or less extent, is a deficit area for all children with ASD and is one of the three features of the traditional triad of impairment together with communication and socialization. Imagination is pretty much synonymous with creativity which is generally described as the physical expression of imagination. Both imply the two skills of flexibility and the ability to think abstractly which are difficult for children on the spectrum. Being creative with art materials means finding a solution to a problem that has no right or wrong answer, and being imaginative means thinking of an idea, if possible, a unique idea, without too much help from an external source. But wait, you might say, I know a very imaginative child with autism. I know many as well, but be careful not to mistake a perseverative interest or a skill with imagination. I have worked with many creative children on the spectrum who simply needed the right interventions to help them express themselves successfully. Art-making is a good vehicle for developing these skills in a child with autism because its tools (art materials) are both visual and concrete; art is both literally and figuratively a useful "drawing board" for the mind's pictures.

Specialized art projects

THE CREATIVE PROCESS

Learning and utilizing the creative process is one of the most far-reaching benefits of art-making. The steps of the creative process involve:

1. Get in touch with your feelings and ideas.

2. Brainstorm possible ways to express them.

3. Experiment with different options and materials.

4. Problem solve your way through the project.

5. Behold the final creation, and

6. Provide an explanation of what you made.

Simply put, it means coming up with ideas and carrying them out. You can walk a child through these steps, which you can give more age-appropriate descriptions like "try it out," "think about it," and "tell me about it." Since the creative process is used for generating new (i.e., anxiety-provoking) projects and ideas, having clear, predictable steps can be reassuring and reduce outbursts of frustration.

NON-VERIDICAL REPRESENTATIONS

Craig *et al.* (2001) used drawing tasks to identify a specific imagination deficit in children with ASD who were described as having difficulty drawing something that doesn't exist in reality (i.e. is "non-veridical"). It is interesting to note that non-autistic, otherwise developmentally delayed children matched for mental age with the ASD-diagnosed participants did not have a significant deficit in this area. Also, participants with Asperger's were less impaired on imagination tasks than their lower-functioning peers, but the impairment increased when the children had to perform spontaneously. Projects such as creating unreal creatures, transformations, or fantastic stories are a good way to practice mental flexibility.

VISUAL SYMBOLS AND METAPHORS

A symbol is something that stands in for something else, for example green represents "go." A metaphor, an imaginative but not literal relationship, is used to suggest a similarity between two things, for example "the TV barked." Use art to make metaphors visual and help the child understand their meaning and function. When the child gets older, you can work on understanding how visual metaphors sometimes hold multiple meanings. Projects might include creating personal symbols to represent the child's interests or using images as metaphors for the child's feelings (e.g., my anger is a tiger, etc.). Work cautiously to make sure that you are not confusing the child as you help him or her to develop abstract thinking skills.

SYMBOLIC PLAY

Symbolic play activities involve abstract and representational thinking when done properly. With small children, it usually means animating and storytelling using objects such as dolls, cars, and so on. Specific types of symbolic play can be distinguished from each other, for example *creative symbolic play* in which arts and crafts are used to create products such as puppets which are then animated or *dramatic symbolic play* (often called "pretend play") which involves acting or taking on a persona or character, like "playing restaurant" or pretending to be a cat. When teaching and modeling symbolic play behaviors, I like to note the child's favorite themes and materials, the length of their playtime (usually, the goal is to increase it), and rate their behaviors along a continuum from least independent to most independent. Ask yourself: Did the child ignore me? Quietly observe? Imitate my actions? Respond appropriately during interactions? Elaborate on a suggestion? Come up with ideas independently?

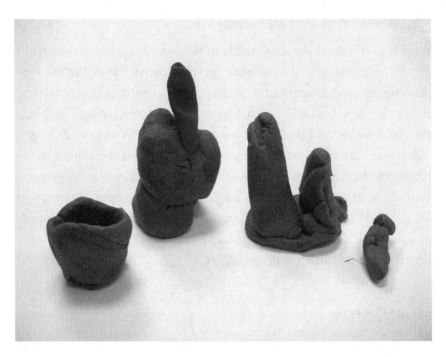

Creative symbolic play: Having a "birthday party" with a three-year-old boy (left to right: cup, cupcake with candle, cake with candles, ice cream cone). Birthday parties can be uncomfortable for children with ASD and it is good to practice how to behave at them.

ABSTRACT REPRESENTATIONS

By this I mean using elements of art such as color, composition, scale, placement, and line to create a pleasing work that is not figurative or does not have other identifiable elements. In other words, it is abstract. This is a natural part of developing aesthetic preferences in neurotypical children (often seen as "doodling" by adults), but children on the spectrum are sometimes a little baffled by it. You can take it to the next level and have the child assign associations with the abstract elements (e.g., blue is cold, jagged line is frustrated, etc.).

SEE ANOTHER PERSON'S PERSPECTIVE

In order to work with the child on understanding another person's point of view, an adult or peer must make art with the child. Not only do children enjoy seeing what adults make, but I believe that seeing another person drawing is akin to hearing their point of view. A child on the spectrum may want to "correct" or change your drawing to make it fit with their preferences, but insist that they respect your work, just as you respect theirs. Help children with theory of mind deficits *see* what you are thinking by making art with them at all possible and appropriate times.

AMBIGUOUS PICTURES

Pictures or photographs that depict vague actions or stories are great tools to help prompt story elaboration and imaginative thinking. You could make your own and then encourage the child to add to the picture or create additional scenes. Ambiguous designs such as scribble drawings, which you can make together, are useful for helping a child imagine an image, much like finding pictures in the clouds.

2. Sensory regulation and integration

Goal

Improve the child's ability to regulate his or her body and integrate sensory experiences.

Children with autism often experience hyper (too much) or hypo (not enough) stimulation due to their body's poor ability to filter sensory input properly and often require adult help to calm or energize themselves. Using art to help them regulate their bodies can be tricky. Often a child will be drawn to materials that match, rather than soothe, their current sensory state, and allowing too much of this can be like putting fuel on the fire and increase their disregulation. It is our job as adults to carefully experiment with the child to determine their response to different materials at different times, and then teach them how and when to use particular materials. A great tool for determining this interaction can be found in art therapist Vija Lusebrink's *Imagery and Visual Expression in Therapy* (1990). Lusebrink puts art materials on a continuum from fluid (wet) to rigid (hard) and claims that the different sensory experiences of the materials interact with a client's symptoms and impact the content of the artwork produced (see Tables 5 and 6). Lusebrink did not create this theory specifically for clients on the spectrum, but it works beautifully with the needs of children with ASD. Sensory integration is a term that is often used loosely and refers to any activity that strengthens mind–body connections and works to reduce defensive or avoidant behaviors toward sensory experiences.

Table 5 Lusebrink's fluid to rigid art materials continuum for two-dimensional artwork, as adapted by the author for children with ASD.

Table 6 Lusebrink's fluid to rigid art materials continuum for three-dimensional artwork, as adapted by the author for children with ASD.

RIGID ↑		RIGID ↑	
	Pen (ballpoint)		Stone
	Mechanical pencil		Wood
	Colored pencils		Styrofoam
	Graphite pencil		Sculpey (oven-bake clay)
	Crayons (wax)		Plasticine clay
	Watercolor crayons		Silly putty
	Charcoal pencil		Plastic Roc (air-dry clay)
	Chalk (sidewalk)		Model Magic (air-dry clay)
	Charcoal sticks		Playdoh
	Chalk pastels		Natural clay
	Oil pastels		Flour-based doughs
	Markers		Papier mâché
	Paint pens		
	Watercolor tray		
	Acrylic paint		
	Tempera paint		
FLUID ↓	Finger paint	FLUID ↓	Shaving cream

Specialized art projects

INDIVIDUALIZE PROJECTS TO IMPROVE REGULATION

Which materials help soothe a child and help them produce their best work is a case-by-case decision. Does the wetness of paint overstimulate an already disregulated child? Does the intense tactile experience of clay distract the child from using it properly; could the child benefit from a less wet or messy clay, or from maintaining some distance by holding a tool or brush instead? Experiment and compromise with the child. Incorporate visual aids and adaptations as needed to encourage independent choices (Chapter 6). Children on the spectrum often get "stuck" in the kinesthetic pleasure of using art materials and are slow to move into representational work. Unless you are practicing scribbling or doing motor exercises I would recommend avoiding disorganized scribbling and insist on some level of control in the child's work when working on improving regulation.

INCORPORATE THE FULL BODY INTO ART-MAKING

Body tracing, body painting, mask making, and creating and wearing costumes or body puppets are big crowd-pleasers among neurotypical kids. Children with ASD often need a great deal of support, encouragement, and structure in order to have a positive experience with these activities due to the great imposition they put on the child's physical and sensory boundaries. If these activities are relevant to the child's treatment goal (either sensory regulation/integration or imagination/abstract thinking), then introduce them with patience and lots of reinforcement.

INCREASE MATERIAL EXPLORATION AND REDUCE SENSORY DEFENSIVENESS

This usually happens as a by-product of art-making, but you might have to do it with intention, particularly for a lower-functioning child.

Present the child with a variety of textures, pressures (applied to different materials), scents, and sounds. Yes, art materials have smells and make sounds! Tasting is usually not a good habit; find another outlet for those needs. Almost all autism therapists address tactile defensiveness, but with art-making there is a product to focus on beyond the material itself.

3. Emotions/self-expression

Goal

Use art to externalize and process thoughts and feelings.

It isn't easy to be a kid on the spectrum. ASD symptoms exacerbate everyday conflicts and make activities that help a child pinpoint and process their emotions very practical. For children on the spectrum, therapeutic art projects provide the concrete, visual format that allows you to literally wrap your hands around a topic. Due to the child's social deficits, the traditional "triangle" of art therapy (the three-part relationship between the child, the art, and the therapist) allows art to act as what art therapist David Henley (1992) calls a "buffering agent" to soften and facilitate the interaction between client and therapist. For kids on the spectrum, I like to call it a *concrete conduit*. Also, current studies suggest that children on the spectrum have an easier time processing objects than faces, and many people with autism testify to this, so in theory the art object may be more useful than the adult's words. The artwork functions as a product that a child can refer to over time as a way to remember and strengthen learning.

In therapy, the way that art projects are determined for this treatment goal is through the "therapeutic relationship," the unique relationship between client and therapist that is a powerful tool in and of itself. Within this relationship, it is the therapist's responsibility to be accepting without condoning, caring without patronizing, and challenging without demanding, and, in the case of an art therapist, to be observant and supportive of the child's artwork. Parents and teachers can also form this kind of bond with a child. Keep in mind that art-making can be either illustrative (e.g., intentionally depicting an event or feeling) or illuminating (e.g., the adult and/or child notice reoccurring themes in the child's artwork). *Any* topic can be turned into an art project by a creative adult. A good relationship often means letting the child take the lead whenever possible and waiting for the teachable moments in which you come up with a project together on the spot. As with other treatment goals, it is important that the adult makes art too, in this case as feedback, or as a way to synthesize or summarize learning. How simple or sophisticated your topic or project will be depends upon the child's mental age and abilities.

Specialized art projects

Any art project that addresses issues that arise from the child.

Common issues include stress-reduction, attachment issues, identifying emotions and connecting them to activities/experiences, developing relational skills, family/sibling/peer relationships, transitions such as entering school or puberty, anxiety, depression, bullying, safe expression of "bad" or negative feelings, understanding and coming to terms with disability, self-esteem, self-awareness, self-management of symptoms, and more. Some of these issues are particularly relevant for children with Asperger's or high-functioning autism. Children of early intervention age can work toward developing a basic "vocabulary" of emotions, how to draw/represent them, and then, as they get a little older, make the connection to real-life experiences.

4. Developmental growth

Goal

To display age-appropriate drawing ability, fine motor skills, overall artistic development, and any relevant deficit area that can be addressed using art.

Clearly this category is a bit of a catch-all, and includes artistic developmental growth and any developmental goal that can be addressed using art projects.

Specialized art projects

FINE MOTOR DEXTERITY

Any art project can tackle this objective. Select a project according to its dominant motor activity (e.g., collage = scissor use, beadwork = pinching, clay tools = cutting, knifing, etc.) and practice, practice, practice! Having an art project to focus on beyond the motor activity required to accomplish it makes work less stressful.

VISUAL SEQUENCING

Sequence drawings (drawing one "frame" of the action at a time) can help break down real-life situations and make them easier to analyze or retell. Comic book formats provide a nice visual structure; Carol Gray's *Comic Strip Conversations* (1994), tailored specifically for people on the spectrum, uses thought and text bubbles to "show" what people are thinking during social interactions.

DEVELOP OR IMPROVE REPRESENTATIONAL DRAWING SKILLS

If making age-appropriate art is the goal, then understanding artistic developmental theory (see Chapter 2) is necessary to determine where a child is at compared with where they should (more or less) be for their age. Unfortunately, "age-appropriate" artwork in the field of developmental disorders often means therapists and teachers devising art projects that help a child's work *look* more age-appropriate, but without any real growth. Be patient and help a child progress along the developmental path without skipping or rushing any critical learning periods. Many of the techniques suggested in the "How to move past

Visual sequencing: Make a comic strip to help sequence and process real-life events.

scribbling" section of Chapter 2 are helpful even if the child is already past scribbling but still delayed for his or her age.

FACE PROCESSING AND SELF-AWARENESS

Portraits are a great way to work on self-awareness by drawing your-self, or to practice interacting with and processing the faces of others by drawing other people from life, as well as work on relationships, understanding self vs. others, and personal space (Martin 2008).

VISUAL MEMORY

You can help a child work on improving long- and short-term memory recall by recording events through drawing in a visual journal or notebook.

SOCIALIZATION AND RELATIONSHIPS

Use art to share (e.g., gift giving), celebrate (e.g., holiday, seasonal, or ethnic traditions), or simply "make special" (Dissanayake 1995). Joint tasks (working together with a peer or adult) can be structured to help practice social skills and turn-taking. Projects such as family drawings and portraits can be used to depict and celebrate relationships. Enhance Social Stories™ with illustrations. Social Stories™ is a specific writ-ten format developed by Carol Gray and Abbie Leigh White (2002) to help people with autism understand social situations. Art projects designed for use specifically within a social context can be found in Appendix A.

META-REPRESENTATION

Those of you who are professionals working with children on the spec-trum might have noticed that I do not include communication as a major treatment goal. While it is one of the major deficit areas for children with autism and a huge area of concern, I think art is best at facilitating self-expression or meta-representation (that which is more complex than or beyond words). Communication implies a much more immediate, practical need to interact with others, and in a world that uses words, drawing is an inefficient substitution. Sign language, picture cards, and communication devices (outlined in Chapter 6) are the usual and useful "plan B" for children who are unable to develop speech and/or written communication. If a child does use drawing to communicate (e.g., drawing a picture of a cup when thirsty) that's great, but in general I feel that the term communication, which has a specific connotation in the field of ASD therapies, is often used too loosely and interchangeably with the more generic term self-expression. A picture speaks a thousand words—and should be encouraged to do so.

5. Visual-spatial skills

Goal

To improve the child's ability to negotiate and render/model in both two- and three-dimensional space as well as the ability to mentally rotate objects.

For many individuals with autism (notably those with savant drawing skills), visual-spatial skills are a strength area, but for others, the development of these skills can be frustrating. I have seen very little middle ground: either it is very hard for the child or they have prodigious visual-spatial ability. If this is an area of strength, then art-making might be an attractive way to address other deficit areas with the child, such as emotional self-expression or socialization.

Specialized art projects

DRAWING EXERCISES

Any drawing project that is specifically designed to "exercise" the brain can be useful. The field of art education has many good ideas, including the classic text *The New Drawing on the Right Side of the Brain* (Edwards 1999), which can be tailored nicely to help children with autism improve their visual-spatial skills and flexibility. Projects might include drawing with their eyes closed, drawing upside-down images, drawing different views (including the side/profile, back view, and views from above and below), more advanced perspective drawing (for older children), or drawing with the non-dominant hand.

SCULPTURE

Modeling clay "in the round" (i.e., taking care to model all sides of the figure, not just the front) means negotiating three-dimensional space. In my experience, children of all ages on the spectrum typically prefer two-dimensional work because it can be kept cleaner, is limited to a single plane/working surface, is more immediate, and usually more colorful. Starting with bas-relief sculptures (flat-back) or drawing visual instructions for the child to follow while modeling clay are both useful interventions to bridge the child's move from two-dimensional to three-dimentional work.

PRINTMAKING

Making prints is the most straightforward two-dimensional art process that requires mental rotation. In order to print a readable image, the plate/stamp must first be carved or drawn backwards. Demonstrating for the child and providing a mirror can help (see Chapter 5 for more about printmaking).

6. Recreation/leisure skills

Goal

To develop productive, enjoyable leisure activities and generalize them to the home and other natural environments.

This treatment goal is probably the number-one reason why parents enroll their children in art activities. Parents desperately want their children to learn healthy ways to happily spend their time (not just watching videos or playing on the computer all day) and desire services that are both therapeutic and recreational, like creative arts therapies, adaptive sports, and hippotherapy. Keep this in mind if you are a creative arts therapist and ever feel pressured to make art or music projects appear more "serious" and are tempted to tone down their playful aspects. Autism therapists in other fields try to incorporate art, music, and movement into their work all the time in order to make it more fun and enhance learning. Pleasure is important for a small child in order to learn from and feel safe with you. Although this is not necessarily a treatment goal that will get me very far with insurance companies, the longer I work with children on the spectrum the stronger I feel that healthy recreation is one of the most important goals of all. Making art offers the child with autism a socially appropriate way to nurture their need for perseverative interests (called "passion" or "drive" in a neurotypical artist), solitude, and visual stimulation, as well as an opportunity for mastery and enjoyment. Be sure to work toward independent art-making in a non-controlled setting, such as with peers at a community art center or at home.

Specialized art projects

Any enjoyable and productive art activity.

Remember, art is the engine that drives treatment goal progress. Art projects are infinite in kind and number and can be created to address any goal, including goals that are often significant areas of concern for children with ASD, such as communication, reading, sequencing, socialization, and flexibility, but not listed as major goals in this chapter. Chapter 4 highlights the six treatment goal areas that I believe are *best* addressed through art-making, since art is usually just described in terms of what it is complementary or adjunct to, instead of asserting its own areas of primacy. Art projects are regularly created or co-opted by teachers and therapists of all kinds in order to achieve success, and rightly so.

Table 7 Summary of Chapter 4.

Goal:	SPECIALIZED ART PROJECTS
Imagination/abstract thinking	Non-veridical representations
	The creative process
	Visual symbols and metaphors
	Symbolic play
	Abstract representations
	See another person's perspective
	Ambiguous pictures
Sensory regulation and integration	Individualized projects that improve regulation
	Incorporate the full body into art-making
	Increase material exploration and reduce sensory defensiveness
Emotions/ self-expression	Any project that addresses issues that arise from the child
Developmental growth	Fine motor dexterity
	Visual sequencing
	Develop or improve representational drawing skills
	Face processing and self-awareness
	Visual memory
	Socialization and relationships
	Meta-representation
Visual-spatial skills	Drawing exercises
	Sculpture
	Printmaking
Recreation/leisure skills	Any enjoyable and productive art activity

5

Tools of
the Trade

The art in art therapy is much like cheese on broccoli: it makes hard work more palatable for kids. Whether or not a clay project is designed to help children with autism calm and regulate their bodies or practice storytelling are distinctions that are usually lost on the child. They are just excited that they get to use clay! This chapter provides you with a tried-and-true list of art materials that are useful when working with children on the spectrum. Potentially any media or project could be used to address any of the six goals outlined in the previous chapter. This is always up to the discretion of the individual adult and child. There is no limit to the possibilities of projects that can be created out of art materials other than the child's ability and interest.

When making art with children with autism, it is important to be confident in your handling of the materials and knowledgeable of their properties. Being both young and on the spectrum, the child's attention span will be brief and if you are slow or insecure with the materials it will impact the quality of your time together. In early intervention, fluidity with art materials and on-the-spot projects are more important than projects prepared in advance. For times when prepared projects are appropriate (for older children or in a group/classroom setting), the recommended reading section at the end of the book will point you toward several useful resources. If mouthing or pica (eating inedible

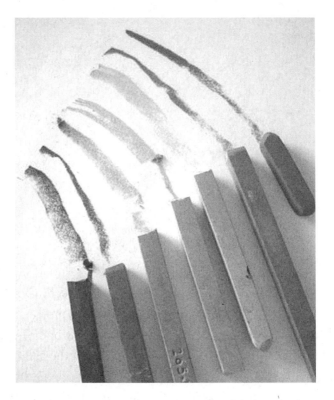

Having a variety of attractive and appropriate materials on hand will make the task easier and more productive for both you and the child.

things) is a problem or if the child has allergies or is on a special diet, you will need to know what is in your materials. Using all non-toxic materials and water-based paints is a good rule of thumb. Check out Monona Rossol's book *The Artist's Complete Health and Safety Guide* (1994) and be sure to read labels when at the arts and crafts store.

I have divided the chapter according to processes ("painting," "drawing," etc.) and then list recommended materials ("pencil," "paintbrush," etc.) for each process. *Immediate processes* (painting, drawing, and clay modeling) are given more attention than *step-intensive processes* (sculpture, mixed media, photography, printmaking, found objects, and collage) because they are more age-appropriate and satisfying for children not yet of school age. Step-intensive projects, supported by step-by-step visual instructions if needed, are great for expanding the child's length of art play and can result in a more finished product, but they are more sophisticated and difficult for a young child, so use them sparingly at first, or you will end up doing most of the work yourself.

Early intervention is the age at which children are given "pre-art" materials such as beans, shaving cream, and uncooked pasta. I have found that pre-art materials can be useful in art projects at any age or level of skill, and that young children do not need preparatory media experience but can pick up a paintbrush or crayon as easily as a bean or noodle and understand its function (perhaps even easier than understanding the function of a food item in art-making). I do not believe that pre-art materials are either primary to a child's art experience or an inferior art material.

As for the quality of art materials that you offer a child, it is hard to justify buying expensive, professional-grade materials for any child due to the large volume that they can burn through, but I encourage you to avoid low-grade "kid-art" materials. Student-grade materials cost a little more than the traditional low-quality finger paints and construction paper, but are superior in manageability and quality and cost less than professional materials. Decide where you want to invest your money. For example, decent quality paper means that their artwork will not disintegrate or fade away in a few years (or even weeks), while the lead in fancy drawing pencils will not last any longer than the lead in a basic yellow #2 pencil. It is good to have some cheap stuff on hand for practicing, but in general shoddy materials like scratchy paintbrushes and lumpy paints make for shoddy work. We want the child (and the child's family) to keep the artwork and be proud of it.

If needed, adaptive tools (brushes, scissors, etc.) can be found in catalogs or online, and often times making your own (if possible) is the quickest, cheapest, and most individualized way to go. I would not be inclined to use them unless the child's therapist or teacher determines that the child needs them. Motor impairment is not a feature of autism per se, and when children are young it is best for them to be taught conventional ways of gripping materials first. It is normal for a small child to experiment with different ways of holding tools and, as long as it is age-appropriate for them to do so, I wouldn't discourage it. If a child with autism persists in holding tools in an improper or unsafe manner, it is usually not because they are incapable of doing otherwise, but because they have become comfortable with it and are resistant to change.

Painting

In my experience painting is far and away the most desirable process to children on the spectrum and the most likely to trigger regulation problems. Managing their passion for paint and their tendency to use it in perseverative or self-stimulatory ways is a lot of work, but worth it for the enjoyment that healthy, age-appropriate painting can bring. The colorful and fluid nature of paint can be exciting, even overwhelming,

Finger painting: A love–hate relationship for kids on the spectrum. Either it is overstimulating and uncomfortable to have on their hands or they want it everywhere!

Table 8 List of useful painting materials.

- Tempera paints (in bottles); for painting on paper

- Acrylic paints (in bottles or tubes); for higher quality painting and painting on wood or dried clay

- Watercolors (in trays); dried cakes of paint are less messy than bottled paints

- Water cups (assortment)

- Brushes (variety of sizes, synthetic or natural hair, both flat and round tips a must)

- Sponges (with and without handles)

- Finger paints (in bottles); low-grade quality for work that probably will not be kept

- Paint rags; cloth rags are more durable than paper towels and create less garbage (wash them periodically)

- Paper (various sizes, colors, and weights, should be strong enough to hold paint)

- Masking tape

- Cardboard and posterboard (either to put under paper or use as a painting surface itself)

- Paint trays/palettes (ones with holes for individual colors, like plastic egg cartons, work best)

- Food dyes (a few drops in water make a simple watercolor "paint" that is generally no big deal if eaten)

- Canvas (loose or stretched); nice for a special project

- Roll of butcher paper/craft paper (good for protecting walls and work surfaces or mural painting)

- Child-size apron or old, oversize shirt

- Face/body paints

---

for small kids on the spectrum. Help them manage their feelings and sensations around paint by providing structure, appropriate timing and length of work time, and behavioral interventions (see Chapter 6) while teaching appropriate use, representation and imagination skills, and having fun. Encourage experimentation with a variety of paint and brush types as well as workspaces (standing at the easel or wall, sitting at a table, crouching on the floor) and sizes (from small to large wall paintings or murals).

Drawing

Drawing is the most basic, primary, and useful of all art processes. Drawing is usually a regulating activity, but depending on the individual child–material interaction, it might not be. Drawing is an immediate tool of self-expression, with no significant set up or clean up needed, and is handy as communication from adult to child when it is

Oil pastels: Faster and more fun than crayons, but beware! Smooth and oily textures can trigger compulsive feelings. (Recognize this face? It's Elmo.)

Table 9 List of useful drawing materials.

- Pencils (various hardness/softness)

- Erasers (pink, white, kneaded)

- Colored pencils

- Wax crayons; break them into nubs to encourage three-point/tripod grip

- Oil pastels (also called cray-pas or oil crayon); much smoother than crayons and require less pressure. Beware of mouthing: they are oil-based

- Markers (all sizes, washable or not)

- Paper (various sizes, color, and weight)

- Sketchbooks; great way to keep drawings together and thumb through like a book or journal

- Dry erase board (plus markers and eraser); fun for quick sketches and saves paper

- Pencil grippers; to encourage three-point/tripod grip if helpful. Can make your own with a little air-dry clay

- Magna Doodle, or any drawing toy of interest

- Sidewalk chalks; sturdy for drawing on rough surfaces

- Chalk pastels; more delicate and for drawing on paper

- Roll of butcher paper/craft paper; good for large wall drawings or body tracings

- Ink pens (ballpoint, felt-tip)

- Ruler, protractor, compass (for older kids) or any straight-edge tool

- Creams or foams (like shaving cream); good for smearing around and drawing in with fingers or a tool

- Watercolor pencils (can wet the paper or the pencils for cloudy, smeared effects)

hard for the child to hear or focus on spoken instructions. The variety of possible drawings is endless. Drawing is the one art process that almost every type of therapist (behavioral, occupational, etc.) engages their clients in at some point because of its important relationship to writing and fine motor skills. Although I do not think that the way a child holds a tool has to be 100 percent uniform with the way in which everyone else holds it (especially when they are pre-school age), you will want to avoid a fist grip.

Clay modeling

Clay modeling is great for exercising little fingers, arms, and shoulder muscles and for naturally engaging in symbolic or pretend play. Teach

Plasticine clay can really take a beating, and even seems to improve the more it is worked. Here is an adorable little squid.

Table 10 List of useful clay materials.

- Plasticine clay (several colors); a durable clay that won't dry out, great for exercising small fingers and sticks together well. Watch out for mouthing (it's oil-based)

- Playdoh (several colors); generally safe if eaten in small quantities, dries out easily and loses its plasticity quickly. Usually contains wheat; watch out if the child is on a gluten-free diet

- Air-dry clay; there are a variety of options to choose from. Having an option to work wet (like Plasticroc) or dry (Crayola) is nice so kids can decide how messy they want to get. Usually comes in white or grey. Can paint it once it is dry (dries overnight)

- Natural earth clay; a lot like playing in the mud to small kids. Kind of impractical to have unless you have a kiln in which to bake the clay. Great for work with older kids

- Oven-bake clays (like Sculpey); can be baked in a conventional oven at home and hardens nicely. A bit pricey and difficult to work for small kids, better for older children. Will need to hollow it out or have a foil armature inside the clay so thick sections don't crack or shatter in the oven

- Homemade doughs; can find different recipes for this online (are usually not much more than making a pie crust). Doesn't hold its shape, but can be a fun option to help a kid get started

- Clay knives and tools (plastic or wood). Not really sharp (some actually quite blunt), for cutting, shaving, poking, and carving. Popsicle sticks are a safe option for young kids

- Cookie cutters, clay molds, extruders (Playdoh brand), and any toy or tool for fun

---

children the basic modeling skills to give them the tools to express themselves three-dimensionally if they don't already know how. There is a great deal that a child can do with only three basic forms: a ball, a "snake" (cylinder/shaft), and a "pancake" (flattened lump). You can make almost anything that a pre-school-age child would want with these building blocks. Also, it is useful to know three different modeling techniques: adductive (add onto a lump of clay), reductive (carve away from a lump of clay) or bas-relief (model in a way that is only seen in two-dimensional space; in other words, the back side is flat). Bas-relief is often a good way to start for children with visual-spatial difficulties. These children have a hard time modeling "in the round," that is, turning the clay over in their hands and modeling other sides or views. Pinch, pull, pound, roll, rub, twist, stick, poke, slap, and squeeze are the primary fine motor skills that they will learn through the enjoyable process of modeling. Check out David Henley's *Clayworks in Art Therapy* (2002) for therapeutic project ideas.

Sculpture

Any act of building or modeling in three-dimensional space can be considered sculpture. A few favorite projects include puppetry/doll-making (any distinction between the two is irrelevant at this age) and mask making. Yarn dolls, tape and foil dolls[1] (made by wrapping tape around a piece of foil pinched in the shape of a figure), wrap dolls[2] (made by wrapping yarn around a piece of cloth pinched in the shape of a figure), paper cut-outs, sock puppets, and stick puppets are all great doll projects. For mask making, you can buy pre-fabricated ones at the store to decorate, use a generic face mold and lay strips of plaster or papier-mâché over it to dry, sculpt it with clay, or just use paper. I would not recommend trying to cast the child's face.

Found objects

"Found objects" simply describes the use of random, non-art materials in an artwork. It really belongs under sculpture, but I wanted to list it as a process in and of itself to highlight its usefulness in developing

---

1   Taught to me by Don Seiden, founder of the art therapy graduate program at the School of the Art Institute of Chicago (SAIC).
2   Taught to me by Barbara Fish, also an instructor at SAIC.

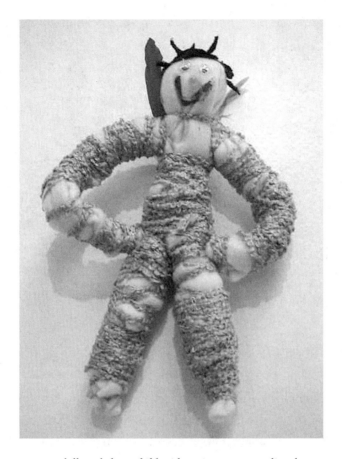

A wrap doll made by a child with autism spectrum disorder.

imagination skills. It is, in essence, the act of turning trash into treasure. We take it for granted when neurotypical children make boats out of cardboard boxes or sculpt their mashed potatoes into a mountain, but when children on the spectrum are not doing this, it can really stand out in contrast to their peers.

Printmaking

Printmaking is, fundamentally, the act of inking an object and stamping it onto paper. Kids love store-bought stamps, but turn this into an art project by helping them make their own (cut-out Styrofoam shapes,

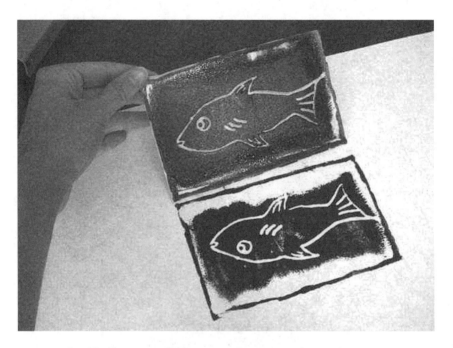

An example of "pulling a print" during Styrofoam printmaking.

carve a potato, etc.). One easy project involves drawing with a pencil into a piece of Styrofoam, rolling ink onto it, then stamping or "printing" the Styrofoam plate onto a piece of paper. Painting onto a surface that will not absorb liquid (Plexiglass or a table top) and then laying paper over it to "stamp" it is fun. This would be called a "monoprint," meaning one, unique print. Printmaking is difficult because, unless your image is perfectly symmetrical, your image will print in reverse (a mirror image) of what you drew on the plate. Printmaking is good for practicing mental rotation or "flipping" images in your head. A great book to get is Lucy Mueller White's *Printmaking as Therapy* (2002).

Collage

Collage simply means cut-and-paste projects. Collages using magazine pictures or torn-paper collages (gluing different colored pieces of paper or tissue together) are common. Just pick a topic and go for it.

Mixed media

Mixed media refers to using two or more media in conjunction, traditionally in two-dimensional format. Most common projects include painting plus drawing, or collage plus drawing. Children will probably do this without even thinking about it.

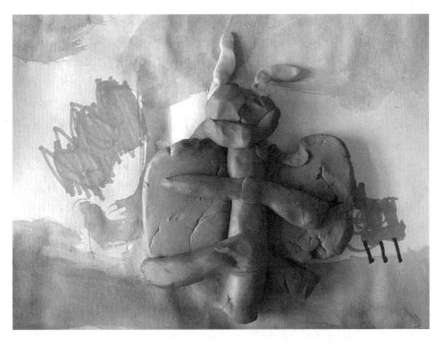

A mixed media project incorporating watercolors, markers, and plasticine clay.

Photography

Snapping photos and pasting them into artwork can be lots of fun. Young children might not remember what they have made from week to week, so waiting to develop film is not ideal. Digital cameras (if you can print where you are working) and Polaroid cameras produce quick images that can be used immediately. Draw on them, incorporate them into mixed media or collage works, or make an album. The digital camera itself is a great tool to help the child identify their interests, by taking a picture of favorite people, items, or places, and incorporate them into art-making by using the pictures on the screen as a visual prompt to copy.

The steps involved in a step-intensive project will be what you and the child create. There are no rules when it comes to being creative. But if you are not already an artist, art educator, or art therapist and these projects seem foreign to you, there are many books and websites to learn from or, best of all, local art classes you can take.

When kids get a little older and begin to favor certain materials, you might consider teaching them about the history and specific techniques of their favorite material. Introducing them to pictures and stories about artists, both contemporary and historical, who excel in their medium of choice, can be both educational and therapeutic if presented in an appropriate manner. For example, I once introduced a boy with developmental disability held in a juvenile detention center to Jackson Pollock's splatter paintings. We had enjoyed painting together in art therapy for a while and had a solid relationship; I waited until I felt sure that this type of painting would be illuminating and tension-releasing for him. If presented prematurely it might have been very destabilizing or confusing. Within the boundaries we set in the art room, he freely enjoyed painting in this manner. Pollock's paintings were presented to him as art history and through the process of mimicking Pollock's style he was able to independently make and articulate the connection to the chaos in his own life.

Also, incorporating other creative arts (especially music and dance/ movement for young children) into art projects as much as possible can enrich the child's experience. Painting to the melody of a song, using a rhyme or story to help brainstorm drawing ideas, or dancing with a homemade puppet help animate and liven up art-making. A little music and dance will provide some gross motor balance to an otherwise heavily fine-motor-based therapy. Resources can be found in music therapy, dance therapy, or adaptive arts education literature.

Table 11 List of useful art materials.

Sculpture materials

- Plaster (in bucket or plaster-coated gauze strips)
- Sand, fine and rough grain
- Powders and gels, for fun or decoration
- Buttons and beads
- Yarn
- String (kite string or twine works great)
- Cloth strips
- Feathers
- Felt
- Cotton stuffing or cotton balls
- Shaving cream
- Balsa wood
- Wood scraps
- Various glues (white Elmer's glue stick, hot glue gun for adult)
- Masking tape
- Aluminum foil
- Papier mâché
- Pre-fabricated items (like generic masks)
- Exacto knife (for adult)

Found objects

- Items from nature (rocks, leaves, sticks, flowers)
- Cardboard tubes and shoe boxes
- Leather or plastic scraps
- Bottles and jars
- ANYTHING safe and useful

Collage

- Magazines (nature or science ones usually have the best photographs)

- Scissors, for little fingers

- Colorful papers

- Glitter

- Any writing or painting materials and glue

Printmaking

- Styrofoam sheet or tray (can order them from art catalogs but the little trays that are used to package vegetables work too)

- Pencil or other pointed tool

- Brayer ("roller")

- Water-soluble printing inks

- Stamps (store-bought or make your own with Styrofoam, wood, potatoes, etc.) and inkpad

- Surface that won't absorb paint or water (a little sheet of Plexiglass is perfect)

- Acrylic or tempera paint and brushes

Photography

- Digital or Polaroid cameras allow you to view images immediately

6

Advice to Help Ensure a Quality Art Experience

Making art with kids with autism is very enjoyable. It is also a lot of hard work when done properly. This chapter is a compilation of advice for adults who make art with children with ASD of all ages. Although there is a lot of information to absorb, if you read it once or twice and begin to put it into practice, these skills will become second nature to you.

Philosophy

Providing a quality art experience for children on the spectrum presents unique challenges due to the child's symptoms. Addressing and overcoming these challenges is not a difficulty of the work, it *is* the work. Behaviors such as refusing to touch paint (tactile defensiveness), only drawing bulldozers (perseveration/obsession), or an inability to animate puppets (symbolic play deficit) often appear to parents as reasons why their child would not be suited to art activities. Yet when a child is referred for speech therapy, for example, it is not because the child presents outstanding verbal skill, but because of a deficit. The use of therapeutic art tasks must be thought of in the same manner. Art-making is the modality or tool through which we tackle relevant deficit areas (imagination/abstract thinking, sensory regulation/

The author and a young artist learning how to paint.

integration, emotions/self-expression, artistic and fine motor developmental growth, visual-spatial skills, and recreation/leisure skills). A child who loves art and will happily work for hours might make faster progress in these areas, but it is the child who appears oblivious to art materials that just might be in greater need of adult assistance to help them discover their creative potential. Very simply stated, a quality art experience for a child on the spectrum can be described as a three-part relationship comprising:

1. relevant, useful art projects

2. a caring, supportive relationship with an adult, and

3. individualized adaptations to help ensure success.

Until now this book has mostly focused on the art projects; this chapter will help round out the other two parts of the equation.

Setting up your workspace

For a population with a reputation as being inattentive, children with autism can be incredibly sensitive to and aware of their surroundings. Environmental stimuli such as sights (visual), smells (olfactory), sounds (aural), what is within reach (tactile), and even tastes (oral/gustatory) and whether the stimuli is pleasing, neutral, or anxiety-provoking are a huge factor when setting up your space for children with ASD. Striking the right balance between the stimuli in your space and the current sensory state of your child will improve the quality of your time together immensely.

Think of your space in terms of whether it provides low, moderate, or high stimulation. Most art studios or classrooms are highly stimulating—colorful art on the walls, large variety of materials in easy reach, sweet smells in the air, even a snack or drink nearby. However, some children with ASD can become overstimulated and impulsive in such a space. Ideally, your workspace should be large enough so that you can create different spaces to accommodate different sensory needs for optimal learning.

A low stimulation room or space should have blank walls, no materials within reach (bring them in as needed), and cover distracting windows. Low stimulation spaces need not be drab; paint the walls a soothing, cool color, cover the floor with soft carpet or rugs, and lay out cozy beanbags and pillows. Keep tables and chairs at a bare minimum.

This type of space is especially useful for young children who still crawl and tumble on the floor, for highly impulsive or distractible kids, or for any child who needs a break or help with regulating. Low stimulation spaces are more contained and will make art projects easier and more successful as you introduce the child to messier, more difficult projects over time. The less time you and the child have to spend cleaning up, the less frustrated you will both be.

A high stimulation room or space should have a variety of art on the walls, materials within reach that the children are allowed to touch on their own, materials out of reach that require adult supervision, high or locked shelves for wet and fragile projects, and a variety of work stations (age-appropriate easel, age-appropriate table, wall, and floor space). Hard (non-carpeted) floors will make clean up much easier and reduce anxiety about messes. If you have a sink in your space, I would recommend posting clear rules in both words and pictures about how and when the sink can be used. If your sink is elsewhere in the building, keeping small bottles of water and a deep tray to shuttle dirty brushes, etc. to and from the sink will work. Both setting up and cleaning up are important life skills; it is to the children's advantage that you do this *with* them and not for them whenever possible. A high stimulation space is designed to encourage safe, independent work.

If you only have one room, then finding a compromise between high and low stimulation room features and keeping it flexible (being able to bring in or remove furniture/materials depending upon the child's needs) will be important. If you are blessed with tons of space, you could outfit a room for a specific material (high stimulation clay room, high stimulation painting studio, etc.). Be predictable without being rigid in terms of how you store your materials; label boxes and jars to encourage independent set-up and keep things in order for those children who become highly distraught by change. Remember that your ultimate goal is for the child to be able to use art-making skills independently, that is, to *generalize* from the adaptive art room to school and home (often referred to as *natural environments*). Get feedback and observations from the child's parents, teachers, and other caregivers to find out if the child's independent art-making is improving. Going outside to make landscape drawings, rearranging the room, rotating the selection of art projects, or making special trips to kid-friendly museum events whenever possible are great ways to encourage generalization and avoid rigid routines.

For families working at home, I would suggest designating a special place in the house as the "art corner" or "art table" (most families do not have the luxury of an "art room"). Add art-making as an activity on your child's daily schedule or as a special weekend activity. Support and encourage your child at first as you would any other new activity (keep reading this chapter for more specific advice), and gradually fade yourself out as your child becomes more independent. Do not let shyness about your own art skills keep you from making drawings and paintings with your child; most likely this will be an experience you will treasure, whether or not artistic ability runs in the family. If you have difficulty getting started or if your child is frustrated, consult with your child's therapists and teachers for advice.

Suggested materials can be found back in Chapter 5, Tools of the Trade. Your favorite arts and crafts store or art supply website will have most everything you need; school supply catalogs will have good child-size furniture options, and any adaptive tools (special brushes or scissors, etc.) that you cannot make yourself can be found online.

Building the relationship

Your relationship with a child with autism will be unlike any other (and might require a fairly thick skin). Children with ASD will be unable to socially reciprocate with you without training and will most likely be unable to appreciate the progress that they are making in their artwork at first. Even a hug from a child might be their way of seeking the pressure and physical sensation of a squeeze, and it can be hard not to take this personally at first. All this might make your relationship feel a little one-sided, but of course no relationship really is (even with people with ASD). It is important for the adult to respect the nature of the child, both its endearing and not-so-endearing aspects, while at the same time setting clear expectations for improvement and change. It will be the little things that let you know that the child is enjoying his- or herself and beginning to trust you. There are several things that you can do that will help children with autism feel comfortable and let you teach them new skills.

Be flexible

The intensity of the child's autism-related symptoms will cycle over time, with days where they are fairly calm and regulated and days where their self-stimulating behaviors are highly distracting and overwhelming. This will interfere with the child's ability to learn, and projects you had anticipated working on might be too stimulating or difficult on certain days. Placing the same demands on the child each session might not be realistic. Being flexible doesn't mean that you release the child from the demands of a project, it means modifying what you present and how you present it. Break tasks down into their smallest parts and negotiate with the child if you can.

Help children assert some control over their bodies

Working with children whose symptoms are primarily physiological means that a huge part of your time will be spent helping children gain some mastery over their bodies' behavior. By demonstrating that you can help the child regulate their body, you are making it possible for them to trust themselves around you. Also, being able to anticipate stressful situations or environments (avoiding when necessary and engaging in when therapeutic) will make you feel like a safe person to be around. Ways to help children regulate their bodies using art are outlined in Chapter 4 and traditional methods are listed later on in this chapter.

Respect art choices

Although it is your goal to help a child move toward less symptomatic forms of creative expression, respecting the types of behaviors outlined in Chapter 3 is important. Allowing repetitive schemas or perseverative interests *in moderation* or as a reward for good work will go a long way to ensuring that art is enjoyable for kids on the spectrum. Praising all creative acts without judgment will create positive feelings toward making art in the child's mind. Highlighting what is positive (e.g., enthusiastic pounding of clay) and ignoring what is negative (e.g., tasting the clay) can work to shape a behavior, that is, hone it into a desirable behavior. Unproductive or self-stimulatory use of art materials can be casually accepted and then set aside in favor of a more appropriate (and more highly reinforced) art project. Punishment is never appropriate when making art.

Get comfortable with close contact

If you have never worked with a child with ASD before, you might be surprised by how much physical contact they either crave or avoid. Even within a single child, different senses might be hyper- or hyposensitive (receiving either too much or too little input). Children on the spectrum lack the empathy needed to consider how their behavior might make another person uncomfortable and require training to understand the meaning of personal space. Also, depending upon the child, you might be needed to help with toileting or to hold a child acting aggressively. I have had children climb up me, reach in my pockets, butt their heads into my belly, pinch my elbows, touch my socks, and smell me—and that was just to show affection. If you decide to make art with children with ASD, then put on an apron and prepare yourself to be on the receiving end of both appropriate (e.g., hugs) and inappropriate (e.g., pinching) touch.

Let yourself love them

Compassionate love for the child is probably one of the most important yet least discussed aspects of working with children with autism. Working intimately with a child who is disabled requires a great deal of patience and gentleness which will be easier to maintain if it is based on love and based less on the adult's ambitions or goals for the child. An adult who cares for and protects a child is a relief to the child's family. I do believe that love is a factor that can positively impact a child's prognosis (and their art skills).

Beware of burn out

Progress is slow for children on the spectrum, and you might feel bored or frustrated at times. Also, if you are a teacher or therapist and work in the child's home, it might feel a bit *too* intimate. Caring for a person with a disability can make you feel sad, depressed, or even helpless. Watch out for feelings of burn out, and do what you need to do in order to take care of yourself, relax, and express these feelings. If you or your child needs to take a break from working on art skills and goals, take a break. The last thing you want is for art-making to become toxic or stressful to the child.

Socialization and communication

As I stated in Chapter 4, I do not include socialization and communication as one of the six major goals to work on using art because, while you *can* tackle these issues using art projects, I do not believe that art-making is better suited to the job than other interventions. Drawing is, in general, an inefficient way to communicate, although it is an excellent way to express feelings beyond the day-to-day needs and wants. And while you can (and I do) design socialization activities within a creative context, I do not believe that art is a naturally social activity for children. Art is a desirable activity that can make socialization tasks more appealing. Art clearly *best* serves our children in the imaginative, visual, sensory, and creativity domains, which are often *under-addressed* areas for kids with autism.

However, you will work on socialization and communication just by being in a relationship; they are the threads that tie together human interaction. Here are a few tips:

Be knowledgeable about how the child communicates and how to support them

If a child is not (or not yet) verbal, there are a variety of communication systems that the child can be taught to use, including electronic communication devices (you select a picture/button on the screen, which the device then speaks aloud; or, a keyboard which speaks aloud when typed on), Picture Exchange Communication System (PECS) cards (the child pieces picture cards together to form requests), or American Sign Language (ASL). Or the child might only use simple sounds and gestures. Gain the knowledge you need to support the child (learn simple signs, how to use the electronic device, etc.) and make sure that the child communicates appropriately.

Insist on and reward appropriate social behavior whenever possible

Take the extra time needed to gain the child's eye contact, prompt them to use age-appropriate manners (e.g., please and thank you), and demonstrate reciprocity. These are important skills that we should be working to help them improve at all times.

Speak the unspoken

When working with a child with ASD, I feel that it is therapeutic (not to mention courteous) to say what is usually unspoken or understood information between two people. A child on the spectrum has a hard time inferring, sensing the abstract, or looking for contextual clues. For example, I might say, "I want you to do this for me *because…*" or "What you did makes me feel this way *because…*" or, it might be as simple as stating my emotion even when it is clearly (to most people) written across my face. Use natural language (figures of speech, metaphors, etc.) but provide explanation. Verbalizing your own thought processes is a good teaching tool.

"Listen" to their body language

Even if the child is verbal, verbal communication often breaks down when the child becomes stressed or upset, and I like to think of body language as an early warning system. *Look* at what the child is telling you about their ability (or inability) to regulate their bodies and concentrate, and help them express what they need before they regress to using behaviors such as tantrums. You will get very good at understanding the child's nonverbal communication and anticipating/accommodating what the child needs, but its important to wait and insist that they communicate to their best ability. Use visual prompting and cueing to let them know what you observe (e.g., yellow light = warning!); using words or raising your voice often aggravates the situation.

Be creative when it comes to eliciting communication/socialization

The overall goal for all children with autism is to communicate and socialize independently, without prompting. Try to come up with other ways to encourage these behaviors without always having to make verbal demands on the child. Playing dumb (pretending you don't understand until the child produces the desired response), clowning (using high affect and silliness to engage the child), and sabotaging (interrupting or changing an activity to get the child's attention) are some of my favorite strategies. Also, structure an art activity so that the child cannot get the materials they want without going to you or to a peer. Exaggeration of expectations is a great way to facilitate learning for *any* child.

Self-monitor and set a good example

Check yourself to make sure you are not demonstrating the very behaviors that you are working to discourage in your client (like taking things without asking, or not using eye contact, etc.). Setting a good example turns even the adult's behavior into productive teaching time. Also, children with ASD often mimic what adults say in a much more direct or literal way than neurotypical children do, and if nothing else, they will definitely respond to your attitude and energy level.

Culture of the autism family

If you are not a member of an autism family, then gaining an understanding of the context in which the child you work with lives (including the impact of that child's autism on the family) is critical to becoming an effective helper. For this section I have clipped in a few paragraphs from my graduate thesis to do the talking for me. Keep in mind that any description of a culture paints a good overall picture but families that differ from the norm will always exist.

> The culture of children with autism is profoundly impacted by the striking difference between the way they interact with the world and how the world engages with them. As both a child and a disabled person, an autistic boy or girl is often doubly shielded from the world at large by family members. Educators and therapists increasingly encourage the participation of children with autism in integrated cultural activities although the children's social deficits and sensory sensitivity present real frustrations. The culture of those whose lives are touched by autism regularly includes education of self and others about autism, advocacy for

access and research, and negotiation of medical and social services organizations.

Difficulty creating and maintaining social relationships is a defining characteristic of autism. The tools of friendship, such as reciprocity, sympathy, and empathy, are a formidable challenge for a child with autism. The ability to understand oneself and others as thinking beings with minds that hold differing thoughts and opinions, described as "theory of mind," is implicated as a characteristic deficit of people with autism. People with autism are generally most comfortable within an established daily routine and do not seek to bring new people into their private world. The ability to assess the need to adapt behavior according to the person one is with (e.g., stranger vs. family member) as well as understanding the reasons for such discriminations within social situations is typically lacking in people with autism. These traits combine to make it exceedingly difficult for people with autism to either participate in mainstream American culture or to build a culture to nurture or address their own specific strengths and weaknesses (e.g., deaf culture, etc.).

The culture of a child with autism, as for any child, is built around the routine and rituals of the family into which the child is born. Since autism is diagnosed according to behaviors which typically do not present themselves during the first few years of life and cannot be identified in the child's physical appearance, many parents believe they are raising a typical child and feel scared and confused at the onset of their child's symptoms. The culture in which the child was embraced (including its hopes, dreams, and aspirations for the child's future) sits back in shock and denial as its child receives a devastating diagnosis. Families experience a period (which can last from months to years) of mourning for the "loss" of their child and must struggle to find a way to include and incorporate the needs of the "new" child into their lives (Baron-Cohen and Bolton 1993). Just as families with a child born with a more immediately recognized handicap sometimes do, the family with an autistic member may isolate itself from mainstream society either permanently out of shame and fear or temporarily as it tries to redefine itself in terms of its disabled member.

If and when the family is able to move past its grief, a culture can be built around the child that works to capitalize on the child's strengths and interests and provide specialized education. For an American child this typically encompasses school and home as well as ancillary therapeutic and recreational activities if the family has the time and resources to seek these out. Historically, reaching out for professional help has been difficult for parents due to misguided speculation that a child's autism was a result of bad parenting (Bettelheim 1967), specifically the fault of cold and unfeeling "refrigerator mothers." The scientific community's ability to debunk this theory has freed up parents to ally with therapists whose interests lie in shaping the child's behavior, rather than in correcting so-called abusive parents.

Over the last 20 years a sharp increase in both the number of American children who are diagnosed with autism as well as the general public's involvement in autism-related organizations and services (e.g., lobbying, fund-raising, family support groups) has heightened American society's awareness of autism. Chicago-based chapters of national organizations such as Cure Autism Now (CAN)[3] hold annual walks, bike rides, and concerts that involve the public in fundraising efforts for research. Representations of people with autism in the media have helped the public learn to distinguish autism from other developmental disorders. Shifts in the attitude of American culture-at-large towards autism have helped to bring children with autism and their families out of the proverbial closet. Due to inclusive teaching standards and national legislation children with disabilities including autism are increasingly becoming viewed as able to participate in American culture, including the fine arts. Children with autism are often fascinated

---

3   Has recently merged with Autism Speaks (www.autismspeaks.org).

with the visual media of American pop culture (television shows, sports and music stars, cartoon characters, etc.). Their interest in culture primarily focused on its material products rather than its communal or social nature, it makes sense that people with autism be encouraged to make objects and participate in culture on the terms in which they are most capable. The arts being an integral part of the definition of culture (Webster 1962) it is clear that autistic children involved in the creation and display of artwork make a valuable contribution to society (Willoughby 2003). (Martin 2005, pp.24–6).

Ways that you can participate in the culture of the families you work with might include attending conferences, participating in fundraisers, or creating art shows to showcase the children's talent and hard work. Many professionals in the field of autism believe that it is therapeutic for families to participate in the "autism community" at large so that they do not feel alone. But many families, who are of course living with autism 24 hours a day, often find this too difficult or undesirable at times. Family culture is not static, and at any given time a family's pre-diagnosis culture, post-diagnosis culture, and the hoped-for culture in each member's imagination will come into conflict with each other and cause stress. It is the values and beliefs of an individual family culture (more than medical or psychological research) that will ultimately determine how they cope and which therapies or treatments they select for their child.

Keep in mind that even the most loving families might not follow through on recommendations made by professionals, and there are lots of reasons for this. Being both a member of an autism family and a therapist working in the field, I know the frustrations that both sides face. Parents have mixed feelings about seeking help with their child, and it can be difficult to shake off feelings of failure that by bringing in an outsider they have conceded they cannot do *everything* for their child. Family members struggle to retain their pre-diagnosis identities and can have a hard time understanding that sometimes helping the child with ASD means changing the behaviors and habits of the family members to create a more regulating and structured environment. Autism families can become very insular, often for both emotional and practical reasons, and hold onto beliefs that no one outside the family can truly "understand" (which may or may not be true). Therapists and teachers might not realize that the child's family does not have the energy or full knowledge needed to carry out suggestions. Help parents make long-term goals (in the midst of a million pressing short-term goals) and don't lose sight of the fact that the family may be grieving, whether they expose these feelings to you or not. Taking on the role of an empathic collaborator and educator to the family builds solid working relationships and helps ensure that skills gained will continue beyond your time with the child.

Directive vs. non-directive approach

Deciding between a directive approach (providing the child with clear suggestions or instructions for a project) vs. a non-directive approach (having the child make art without instruction to see what happens naturally) is, and should always be, a decision made on a case-by-case (or even moment-to-moment) basis. But in general a directive approach is going to best serve the needs of children on the spectrum. A non-directive approach to art-making might benefit a child with Asperger's or PDD-NOS ("high functioning"), but for most children on the spectrum, non-directive art-making simply will not work. Children in general usually stay on task better with instruction and incentives, and for children experiencing symptoms that interfere with attention span and appropriate art play, it is imperative to create these conditions.

An individualized directive with least invasive prompt as possible is my personal rule of thumb when working with a child with ASD. By "individualized" directive I mean one created in the moment by the adult tailored on all levels (motor, sensory, developmental, and emotional) to the individual child. By "least invasive prompt as possible" I mean providing as little direct assistance as necessary for the child to complete the task. Types of prompting for a child with ASD from least invasive to most invasive usually involve: gesture/point/tap (e.g., point to the paint), verbal prompt (e.g., "get the paint"), visual prompt (e.g., show pictures of how one gets paint), light touch/hold (e.g., light hand on wrist to lead to paint), or hand over hand (e.g., hold child's hands and arms and physically maneuver them through getting paint). If the child needs highly invasive help, then you will want to pair a low-invasive prompt with the high-invasive prompt and then slowly fade out the high-invasive prompt as the child masters the task (e.g., state "get the paint" while helping the child do so hand over hand, then reduce your amount of physical presence over time). Moving from most to least prompting (fading yourself out) or least to most (increasing support as needed) are both effective ways to teach art skills. Keep in mind that the designation "least" or "most" is fairly subjective since some kids, depending on their sensory issues, might find, for example, a verbal prompt more invasive than a light touch or picture. If you are in contact with a behavioral therapist, that person will be a great resource for more specific tips about prompting.

Although directives are important when making art with kids with autism, beware of becoming too formulaic with the child. Common among therapies for children with developmental disabilities is what I call the "workbook approach." Workbooks can be useful tools, especially as "greatest hits" compilations to share with others or as a stimulus to jog your brain when you are stumped for ideas. But when used as pre-planned directives they can become crutches and take your focus off the child. Support the child's art-making process, but do not overly dictate what the child's art product is supposed to be. Over-planning in advance by adults is not necessarily an advantage (especially if you are trying to help the child become more creative and flexible) and children with ASD need such intensive, individualized instructions that any workbook project would have to be altered to adapt it to the child anyway.

Although it might sound antithetical, providing directives and prompts will help a child with autism progress toward independent

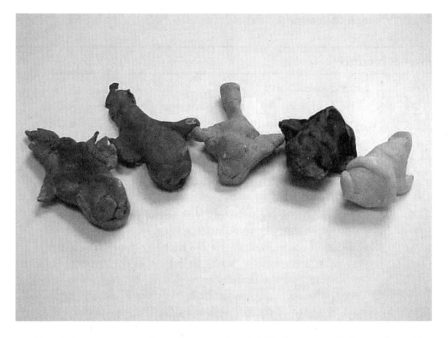

Making fishes using most to least prompt: This child had some tactile discomfort with the wet clay and visual-spatial difficulties with modeling, so I started with lots of hand-over-hand assistance and demonstration and slowly faded it out. The final fish is the most crude but it is the best one of all because the child made it all by himself. Working this way is often less frustrating to the child than having to face the task without clear expectations and then have his work corrected by an adult.

work. By providing structure and expectations you are helping to free up the child from anxieties and thus be more productive. Internalizing prompts (in other words, learning how to self-direct) provides them with a way to organize their minds and bodies and focus less on sensory distractions and more on the task at hand. Gains will come slowly, but give them time to practice and process the information and avoid the temptation to offer more prompts than necessary—it isn't helpful to the child if you do most of the work.

Table 12 Range of traditional prompt types.

Prompt hierarchy:

Most

Hand over hand

Involves taking the child's hands and moving them through the task. The adult is doing the actual work, while the child is experiencing the motor skills they will need to use to eventually do the task on their own.

Light touch/hold

I also like to call this a "regulating touch." Described as an adult providing a gentle touch or holding the child's elbow, wrist, shoulder, etc. to help them keep their movements calm and controlled. Be careful that you are only providing pressure; the child should be doing the work. Sometimes a child might want an adult to, for example, make a drawing for them although they are capable of doing it themself (probably due to need for control or anxiety); giving the child a regulating touch while they draw can be a good compromise.

Visual prompt

Provide a picture or written instructions of the task for the child to refer to.

Verbal prompt

Simply providing verbal direction or instruction (e.g., "Let's paint.").

Gesture/point/tap

Subtle command to cue the child (e.g., tap on the chair for "sit down," point to the easel for "let's paint"). Could be another nonverbal prompt such as facial expression or following one's eyes.

Least

Managing difficult behaviors

When talking about children with ASD, a "difficult" behavior could conceivably include any symptomatic behavior. But here I am referring specifically to self-stimulatory behaviors (such as hand-flapping, visual stimming, humming, rocking, hand-wringing, toe-walking, spinning, etc.) or behaviors that are harmful to the child or to others (tantrums, grabbing, pinching, scratching, hair-pulling, head-banging, fist-banging, punching, biting, etc.). Basically, behaviors that are either intolerable or hinder learning. By knowing your child well, you will probably be able to determine what your child's particular triggers are and how to help them. But for children with autism in general, there are two common reasons for difficult behaviors: communication barriers and/or sensory disregulation.

All children get frustrated and impatient with the communication shortcoming that goes with their young age and immature development, but for children with ASD, this can be doubly aggravating. Make sure that the child has a functional way to communicate needs and frustrations (discussed earlier in this chapter) and watch their behaviors closely. If it is a disregulated sensory system (an over or understimulated body) that is causing the behavior, then evaluate the environment and either add or remove stimulation; teach the child how to self-regulate/self-soothe in a socially acceptable way on their own, if they can. Early intervention is a difficult time for managing behaviors because the child's communication is still immature. Adults are often still pushing for verbal communication and the child is getting accustomed to adults actively and intensely trying to alter their natural (autistic) behaviors. Transitions are hard, change is hard, and no matter how kind and supportive you are, the child may be reluctant to comply with you for a while. You are stirring up their comfort zone, and that is usually unwelcome.

So, how to handle the actual behaviors? Brush up on your behaviorism. Autism is currently defined by behaviors, so it is no wonder that there is a behaviorist thread that runs through many ASD therapies to a greater or lesser degree. Teachers, therapists, parents, and anyone working with children on the spectrum share a host of tools and techniques that come from a body of now-common knowledge that probably originated from both published studies (in fields such as behavior science, rehabilitative therapies, and education) and adaptations created by families out of necessity and shared with others. The choice and implementation of these tools is determined through analysis of the child's behaviors, or simply by asking the question, what is the *function* of the behavior? What is it trying to accomplish at face value? (Art educator Viktor Lowenfeld used similar reasoning when he spoke of addressing a child's *motivation* for art-making.) If you can interpret non-verbal communication, then analyzing behaviors and determining how to handle them is really quite simple. Is the child letting you know that he needs a break? Help them express it appropriately and give them one. Is the child trying to get your attention by being inappropriate? Ignore it. Is the child trying to get out of work to go play with a toy? Insist that they finish first. Use visuals to make sure that your instructions are clear. As with most children, consistency is key in helping your response to the child's behavior have maximum impact. Think of the child's need for sensory stimulation as a physical craving. Probably the only intervention at present that will truly reduce the craving itself is medication, but you can limit, manage, and substitute it through behavioral or sensory techniques. Here are a few suggestions; each child is different and you will have to experiment a bit to find what works for your child.

- take deep, calming breaths

- informal massage (on hands, cheeks, head, etc.)

- joint compressions

- tight pressure/squeeze (burrow into a tight space, sleeping bag, wrap child in blanket and hold, Temple Grandin's "squeeze machine" is available at some therapeutic schools or clinics)

- weighted pressure (weighted vest, weighted blanket, etc.)

- use a timer (egg timer, digital, etc.) or count down aloud/on fingers to prepare for transitions

- provide vestibular input (sensation of vibration/movement) like a swing, riding in a car or on a horse

- darken or brighten the room

- reduce or add auditory input (move to quiet room, play music, give nonverbal instructions)

- fine motor activity (squeeze clay, pound with crayon, etc.)

- gross motor activity (run, jump, tickle, etc.)

- modify therapist's affect (high, playful vs. low, calming)

- snack or drink

- fluid/wet sensory input (lotion, finger paints, water tray)

- nap before session

- preferred regulating activity such as swimming, drawing, yoga, etc. before session

- avoid sensory shocks (e.g., slamming doors, loud vacuum cleaner, shout, etc.)

Keep in mind that just because an intervention helps the child calm down and focus, it does not mean that the child will prefer it (although usually they will at least tolerate it). Preferred activities (such as watching TV, spinning toys, etc.) are often disregulating activities, as they match the child's current sensory state but exacerbate it, and should only be allowed in small quantities. This is easier said than done, but should still be the goal. Art materials can trigger these behaviors too, so if there is a material that is disregulating for a particular kid, keep it out of reach so they do not feel punished for trying to use it. Some interventions listed above will work for one child but not for another and may only work periodically for others. What is calming for one person might be energizing for another; the key is to know the individual child. Ideally, you can use these techniques to help a child transition into work and maintain good behavior, thus preventing any outbursts altogether, but most often they are used for damage control. (See the upcoming Adaptations section for more ideas.)

Managing behaviors means asking children who have no need to please or impress you to change a part of themselves that they might have no motivation or desire to change. Thus, it is so very important to pair or reward self-regulating activities (and all successful work for that matter) with things that are enjoyable and desirable to the child.

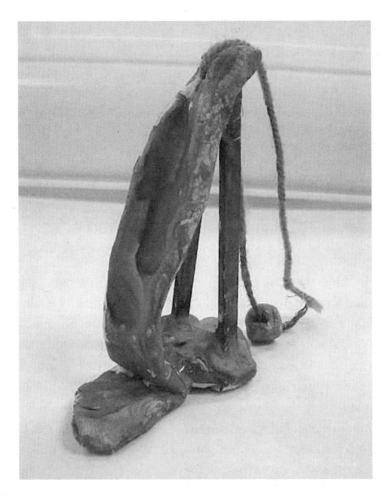

Have the child use art to make their own rewards and to transform perseverative interests: This little sculpture was made by a child who was completely preoccupied by the thought of elevators and water slides for several weeks. I showed him how to make a simple slide with a lift and he was allowed to play with it as a reward for good work (and for not talking about slides and elevators).

Behaviorists call this a reinforcer. Use reinforcers to both strengthen desirable behaviors and systematically decrease negative behaviors. As those of us who took Psychology 101 in college learned, there are two main types of reinforcement: positive reinforcement (when you present something desirable, like a candy or a smile) and negative reinforcement (when you take away something undesirable, like allowing the child to not eat their vegetables or to end work early). Select what works best for your child. As for the items themselves, there are primary reinforcers (food, sensory input) and secondary reinforcers (something that represents something else, like a token that can be traded for candy).

Always pair a reinforcer with social praise (ultimately, you want that to be the only reinforcement necessary) and, ideally, make sure that you have the approval of the family to use primary reinforcers as the child might be on a special sugar-free, dye-free, or gluten-free diet. Make sure that the child does not spend more time enjoying reinforcers than working; it is important to keep the reinforcement time brief so that the child does not get too engrossed in it and then have a hard time transitioning back to work. (Behaviorists actually plot specific intervals of time for reinforcement.) If you are making art with the child you will have a slight advantage when it comes to reinforcement because art is often both work and a prize to a child; either they do not need a reinforcer as motivation, or they might choose a different art project (something perseverative, like painting stripes or rainbows) as the prize. But don't take this for granted because it only works part of the time; you will still need to use non-art reinforcers for many kids. Most professionals and parents utilize at least some behavioral principles nowadays, and applied behavioral analysis is considered to be one of the most successful therapies for children with ASD. It is to our advantage to learn and incorporate behaviorist principles even while working on fun and desirable activities such as art projects. Solid support will ensure that art-making remains enjoyable even as you challenge the child to work and grow beyond their comfort zone.

Adaptations

An adaptation is any useful change made to help facilitate learning, including changes in the adult's behavior, in the environment, and in the materials. Here I want to discuss adaptations that have not been covered elsewhere in the book, mainly, visual adaptations and material

Labeling/ordering: Use visual labels (with pictures and/or words) on your materials and in your workspace to encourage independent work. Even color labeling the environment (e.g., different colored chairs for different parts of the room, different colored cabinets with different functions) can also help. You could even label different workstations within a space to help a child select what they want to do. All this provides the child with a sense of order and aids communication.

Visual boundaries: Providing visual boundaries within both the child's art project (e.g., dividing a piece of paper into a grid, putting masking tape on the table to create a personal space boundary) and the environment itself (e.g., screening off distracting parts of the room) can help improve a child's focus or make an overwhelming task a bit more manageable. Dividing the paper made the topic of "emotions" more manageable for this child.

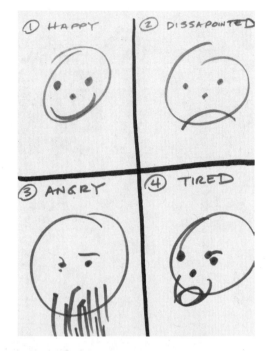

Physical modifications: Make any alterations in materials to encourage proper tool use. Some modified tools can be bought from a store (adaptive scissors, etc.) or make your own (increase the surface area of a tool by wrapping in tape, break a crayon into smaller pieces, etc.). This slant board was made from a three-ring binder. Choosing to work on the floor, at the table, easel, or wall is also a physical modification.

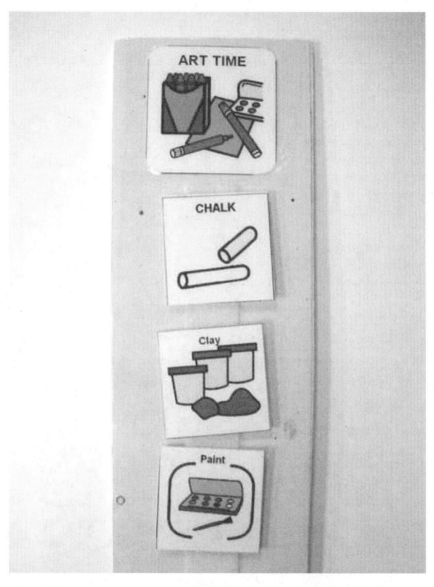

Visual schedules: These will help set expectations and reduce anxiety at transitions. There are a myriad of possible kinds: a visual schedule can incorporate pictures (pre-made or drawn on the spot) and/or words, run vertical or horizontal, incorporate a token system and/or have prizes/sensory breaks interspersed within it, allow the child to interact with it (cross off items, write a summary of an activity, etc.), be lengthy (for the entire session, day, or even week) or short (e.g., first, clay time; then, play break). Keep them organized, clear, and predictable and negotiate with the child if appropriate.

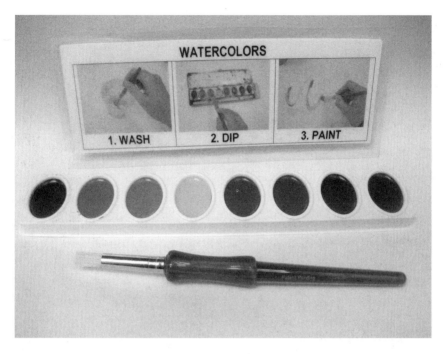

Task planning: Pictures of the steps/sequence required to complete a task can help reduce anxiety and encourage independent work. They can be used for simple tasks like washing a paintbrush or multi-step projects like building a doll. Digital cameras are great for making sequence pictures that are specific and personalized.

modifications. This is a list of tried-and-true adaptations, and not an extensive list, so do not be afraid to come up with creative new ideas. Again, each child is different. None of the ideas here are my own; I would give credit where credit is due if I could, but by now these techniques have become common knowledge, developed and refined by many universities over decades.

Consider all adaptations temporary; the child can become dependent on them and the activities become overly "scripted." Use them until you can downgrade to a less invasive adaptation or prompt. Picture cards can be made from computer software such as Boardmaker®, from taking digital pictures, or draw your own.

Communicating: Even if the child responds well to spoken communication, you might want to pair it with visual language at times. If the child needs help regulating, you might want to cut out auditory input (talking), and if the child's social skills are poor, you may consider using sign/gesture/facial cues to encourage them to attend to you. Know simple signs (e.g., yes, no, please, thank you, more, stop, give me, hello, goodbye, art, paint, colors, etc.) and pair them with spoken language. Keep a large "vocabulary" of picture cards handy that the child can choose from to select activities. Never assume that one mode of communication will be sufficient for the child at all times, even if the child is verbal.

Safety issues

There are times when the behavior of a child with autism is aggressive and dangerous. Not *all* children with ASD are aggressive, but most will act out violently sooner or later. Plan on it. If unable to calm down, a frustrated, scared, angry, or impulsive kid on the spectrum might strike out and claw, slap, kick, hair-pull, bite, or push the perceived source of their aggravation. This might be the therapist making them work, the mother making them eat their vegetables, the doctor trying to bandage their wound, or just the nearest warm body, which is unfortunately often themselves or a caregiver. I do not say all this to scare or alarm you, but it is important not to understate or minimize violent behavior, even if it comes from small children. It is true that they are much easier to handle when they are small, but that tiny (usually, male) body will grow strong, and they need to learn that their behavior is unacceptable *now* while the damage is minimal. Minimal, but not necessarily small, since an aggressive child can critically injure another small child, break an adult's glasses, or cause a parent to crash the car.

If a child is acting aggressively and you have already tried the self-soothing interventions and adaptations discussed earlier as well as a "time-out," "rest time," or any other intervention, and the child is out of

Don't eat it!: Pictures can help make important messages clear (and also save you from having to say it all the time).

control and you suspect will hurt himself, then you may need to hold the child to keep him from hurting himself. Stay calm and don't get angry or raise your voice; be firm, be kind. Look into getting training (probably through a hospital or school) on how to perform proper holds and utilize pressure points if needed. If the child is trying to harm you, it is usually best to leave the situation rather than trying to fend off the child, but stay close enough to keep your eye on the child. Punishment (which typically means loss of reinforcers) is *not* going to help the immediate situation, and in fact you might need to increase the frequency of reinforcement drastically by rewarding every tiny positive attempt to self-regulate to help the child calm down. Ignoring is also not a good idea for obvious safety reasons.

Besides aggressive/self-abusive behaviors, other safety issues you need to be aware of include whether or not the child has seizures and if the child has been known to mouth or eat inedible items ("pica"). Know the family's plan of action if the child has seizures and practice a little to make sure you are prepared. Maintaining up-to-date first aid/CPR certification is strongly recommended. Also, if you are working with older children or adults that you would be unable to lift in an emergency, then it is a good idea to make sure that there are other adults around who can help if needed. As for your art materials, use common sense and do not offer glass, ceramic, or petroleum-based materials to a child with pica. Educate yourself on the ingredients of your materials (check out the book recommended in Chapter 5 Tools of the Trade) and even if they are non-toxic, they are still not food and should not be tasted. Keep in mind that some ingredients can be absorbed through the skin as well, and if the parents have their child on a special diet or the child has an allergy, even touching or smelling some materials might compromise the child.

If you are not the parent of the child, then in violent or emergency situations your first priority should be to keep yourself safe. Compromising your physical integrity is *not* a part of the job as a teacher or therapist, and you will definitely need to budget your energy for your other students. I know that it is hard for caring, self-sacrificing adults to hear this, and even as I write it I do not fully buy it myself; you will feel pressure to be able to "handle" the child and feel defeated if he acts out violently. Be firm with the child if the behavior is task-avoidant in nature, but know your limits and exercise your right to self-preservation. Make sure that parents and co-workers know what to expect from you in these situations (Will you use holds? Will you be uncomfortable?) just as you will need to know what to expect from the child. Minimize possible problems by doing a "pre-flight check" of yourself and your room (e.g., wear contacts instead of glasses, tie your hair back, wear pants, put breakable items out of reach, have reinforcers within reach, etc.) and try not to take it personally; the intent to harm for harm's sake in these children is rare.

Cultural differences

Cultural factors impact children with autism in every way, from the influence of their immediate family to the type and quality of services they receive. How you discipline a child with a disability, what you de-termine to be knowledge worth teaching them, and the sensory input (noise, space, food, etc.) of the home environment are all cultural deci-sions that impact the symptoms of a child with ASD. Even the religious views of the family will influence how the child is viewed and treated. Therapists and teachers encounter cultural differences between them-selves and their students' families and even their co-workers regularly, but do not necessarily identify them as such. Ask yourself, do your rec-ommendations seem practical or worthwhile from the cultural perspec-tive of the child's family? Is my disagreement with my co-worker or the child's parent based on research or on cultural assumptions?

Although ASD does not discriminate when it comes to the fami-lies it impacts, access to treatment is not the same for all children. Socioeconomic disparities and the increasing consolidation of wealth in the U.S. impacts millions of families, thousands of them with chil-dren on the spectrum, and resources impact prognosis. As an American author writing for a Western audience, my cultural assumption is that children with ASD have a right to a quality, specialized education (written into law through the Americans with Disabilities Act) and that professionals in the field have a responsibility to provide it. But might you encounter a family member or professional who believes or acts differently? And who determines what "quality" services are? Regional differences will determine what is considered to be the best treatment for children with autism, and this often grows out of the perspective of the pioneering figures in the region. For example, this book is influenced by the views of behavioral and developmental psychology, while a related book, Evans and Dubowski's *Art Therapy with Children on the Autistic Spectrum: Beyond Words* (2001) is influenced by object relations theory and was written in Great Britain. If both approaches get results, then who is to say which one is more correct?

No matter how well-intended and educated we all try to be in order to help children on the spectrum, culture tints the lens of our perspectives. Make sure that you take this factor into account.

Delicate issues regarding art

Art can be a surprisingly touchy subject. This realization blindsided me when I first started working in the field, as a green art therapist who had a hard time conceiving of art as anything other than positive. First, I think that the general public doesn't know much about art therapy and autism, and in order to try to understand something of which they have little knowledge, people often piece together a misunderstanding. Families of children on the spectrum might think that my job is to psychoanalyze a child's drawings (it is not), and worry that I would misdiagnose their child's developmentally delayed work as indicative of some darker, more psychologically charged disorder than autism. Children's drawings created in therapy are mythologized by the media (even pathologized in horror/suspense films) and it is no surprise that an adult who had little knowledge about art therapy would be wary. Second, a lot of families think that their child can't "do" art. There seems to be a general belief that creativity is something you either have or don't have. Most people only make art as a child (unless they decide to "become an artist") and I hear adults belittle their own drawing skill and creativity all the time. Those who do decide to pursue art-making as a career regularly feel devalued by society and are forced to give it up just to pay the bills. Even artist parents might not realize that art-making is something that they can share with their autistic child.

Last, and most relevant, I think that artwork made by children on the spectrum makes people squeamish because it makes the disability visible, puts their difference on display. It is tangible, concrete, and in your face. Also, drawing might be a bitter topic for a parent whose child can draw well but is not even toilet trained yet, or for a parent who regularly encounters people who think all people with autism can draw like Rain Man and their child doesn't measure up. Try to help families realize that nothing about their child is permanent and that art skills can be learned. Let them know that art is a working surface, the field on which a child experiments, and is a changing, growing, beautiful thing. Help the public see the charm and intensity of artwork made by people with autism by organizing art shows. Help parents understand and recognize their child's progress in the six goal areas outlined in Chapter 4 and how you and their child are using art to address those goals. Art-making, just like language and social behavior, are skills that neurotypical children learn and absorb so easily on their own that we take this for granted. So when a child's disability blocks this natural learning we sometimes forget that these skills *can* be taught.

Is there anyone who could *not* benefit?

Art isn't for everyone. But in my experience art-making tailored to the needs and behaviors of children with ASD can provide real benefits to these children. I have seen children with "no interest," when all they needed was proper structure, blossom into some of the most motivated and high-performing little artists I have seen. I have seen low-functioning and aggressive children make their first organized scribbles once their bodies were regulated and behaviors under control.

I have seen teenagers surprise adults who thought they could not draw simply because as children, the teenagers had never been given the right visual supports or time to practice. So, never say never. Whether the goal is simple or sophisticated, if it enhances the child's quality of life, it is worthwhile.

Do you remember making art as a child? Probably it was fun and full of color, stories, and adult praise. But maybe it was frustrating, full of self-criticism and broken crayons. For better or worse, those early

The author as a young artist learning how to paint.

experiences with art impact the way you view art-making to this day. Now imagine that you are a child whose hands itch with the need to squeeze something, whose eyes seek out color patterns, who screams in frustration when words fail them. A child who *needs* art. Your body struggles against your intentions, the art materials both scare and excite you at the same time, and the adult at your side is not sure of what to do with you.

I was a child who needed art, but I was lucky, being on the other end of the wide spectrum of human ability. I didn't need much help. But when I became the sibling of a person with autism, I think I began to need art even more. Mostly as a private sanctuary for myself, but also as a place to work out feelings that I could not really talk about. Being a "sib" is definitely a mixed bag of fear and joy, worry and hopefulness. Art was like a friend who taught me how to invest in myself, how to turn hurts into tools. Would I be writing this book today if it were not for my brother? I doubt it.

Artists understand obsessions, artists understand sensory needs, artists understand the failure of words. And some little artists happen to have autism. I hope this book has shown you the importance of helping these children access their creativity and given you the tools that you will need for the job.

Creative Community: Group Art Projects for Kids with ASD

This book provides advice and resources on how to facilitate a thera-peutic art experience for young children with autism, which is usually best accomplished at this age by working individually ("one on one") with the child. But once the child enters school, learning how to suc-cessfully socialize with the other children will become an important goal. Art projects can be tailored to work on social skills within a group setting, and the art materials themselves often make this hard work a little more relaxing and enjoyable for the children. Group work at this stage usually requires a clear project planned in advance in order to provide the children with a shared goal. These projects can act as a bridge or stepping stone that moves the child beyond early interven-tion goals and toward more sophisticated work (if and when the child is ready).

In this section I have outlined projects that I have developed and regularly use with early elementary school-age children on the spec-trum. The primary goals are social (artistic skill-building is secondary) and so the children do not have to be able to draw at an age-appropriate level (as long as they can do preschematic level work). Adaptations and visual aids (as outlined in this book) can be used to a greater or lesser degree depending upon the children's needs. When developing new project ideas, be sure to design the activities around goals that encourage physical and verbal interaction, group brainstorming, social-skill building, and friendships—with art-making at the heart of it all. As always, projects are best when designed with specific children in mind.

Project: Group mural (shadow tracing)

Goals: Body awareness, posing, reading body language, and figure drawing.

Materials needed: Large piece of paper taped to the wall and markers (or other drawing materials of your choice).

Directions: Shadow tracing is essentially a body-tracing activity but with less physical intimacy. It is a great way to begin to help the children become more comfortable with close contact. Turn off the lights and invite one child to hold a flashlight while another peer stands in front of the paper, casting a shadow. Invite another child (or do it yourself) to trace this shadow. The child can then fill in the details of their body and clothing (or you could invite the children to fill in the details of their peers). Continue until all children are represented on the mural. Group murals of the children's bodies are a great way for the children to pay attention to and get to know each other; be sure to have a conversation after you finish about each person in the mural.

Project: Group mural (body tracing)

Goals: Body awareness, posing, reading body language, figure drawing, and intimacy.

Materials needed: Large piece of paper on the floor and markers (or other drawing materials of your choice).

Directions: Invite the children to take turns lying down on the paper in the pose of their choice and trace each other's bodies. (This is a great way to work on patience and drawing control.) The children can then either fill in the details of their own body or that of a peer's body. Hang the paper up on the wall after finishing to allow the children a good look at their work and encourage descriptions and storytelling about the figures both individually and as a group.

Project: Group mural (imaginative)

Goals: Imagination and abstract-thinking skills, attention to peers, turn-taking, patience, compromise, and loss of control over the shared drawing/theme.

Materials needed: Large piece of paper taped to the wall and markers (or other drawing materials of your choice).

Directions: Try to avoid providing the children with a theme or topic for their mural and encourage them to come up with one on their own as a group. Have them take turns adding to the mural in a way that works with the theme and encourage the children to let each drawing build from the previous one. This project provides the children with an opportunity to see brainstorming in action as well as presenting opportunities for recall and theory of mind challenges (e.g., "What has he drawn before?" "What do you think he will draw next?").

Project: Portrait drawing

Goals: Selecting and working with a partner, attention to faces, attention to detail, and close interaction.

Materials needed: Paper of any size (8½" x 11" standard) and markers (or other drawing materials of your choice). Watercolor or tempera paints are a nice way to fill in color if you choose to work on larger paper.

Directions: Have each child select a partner to work with and seat the partners facing each other. Instruct the children to draw their partner's face, paying close attention to details that distinguish their partner from the other peers. The children should hold still for each other as needed. Invite them to share their portraits with the other person and get feedback. Watch to make sure that the children are not allowed to "correct" their partner's drawing; each artist's work should be respected. Children who have difficulty with loss of control over how they are drawn can be invited to make a joint portrait, drawing together with their partner, practicing compromise and communication.

Project: Interactive portraits

Goals: Turn-taking, loss of control over the shared drawing, attention to detail, flexibility, and interaction.

Materials needed: Several pieces of paper taped to the wall and markers (or other drawing materials of your choice).

Directions: For interactive portraits, tape one piece of paper to the wall for each child. Have the children draw each peer in succession, taking turns for each body part (i.e., one child draws the eyes, then passes the marker to the next child who draws a nose, etc.). The result will be a "gallery" of creative portraits, each one containing input from every child.

Project: Peer figure drawing

Goals: Body awareness, posing, patience, perspective-taking, attention to detail, and figure drawing skills.

Materials needed: Paper and drawing materials of your choice.

Directions: Seat the children at tables arranged in a circle and invite the children to take turns selecting peers (one at a time) to sit alone as the model in the middle of the table (on a chair, beanbag, or stand, etc.). This model must be able to hold still (more or less) while the other children draw the model, each from their own vantage point. This project requires a great deal of patience and impulse control, so keep drawings quick and build up to a longer pose/drawing time.

Project: Community quilt

Goals: Identifying individual interests, understanding group/community concept, and fine motor skills.

Materials needed: Fabric squares (any uniform size and various colors), fabric paint (in fine-tipped squeeze bottles), and glue.

Directions: Provide each child with a fabric square and allow them to decorate it as they wish with the paint (feel free to use markers, glue on yarn, etc. if able). Once the squares are dry, glue each piece together to form a quilt. (An adult should probably do this with a hot glue gun for best results.) Have the children explore and discuss the different panels of the quilt/the different members of the group.

Project: Friendship boxes

Goals: Memory recall and gift-giving skills.

Materials needed: Small boxes (wood or cardboard; you can often find prefabricated boxes at arts and craft stores), paper and markers, paint (tempera or acrylic) and paintbrushes.

Directions: Allow each child to paint a box and decorate it with personal touches (maybe with photos from group, favorite topics to draw, etc.). Then pass around the boxes one at a time and invite each child to make a drawing especially for each person's box. The drawing should be of or about the person who owns the box. Once finished, each child should have a box filled with drawings from their peers. Friendship boxes are a great project for a group that is ending because it encourages the children to reflect on their knowledge about each peer and provides a tangible collection of memories.

Project: Art show

Goals: To celebrate and showcase accomplishments outside of the group setting.

Materials needed: An attractive, safe space to hang up/display the children's artwork.

Directions: An art show is a wonderful way to summarize and share the children's progress with their families and to help the children understand the social potential of art-making. Be sure to practice in advance show-and-tell skills (such as introducing yourself, describing what you made, and accepting/giving compliments) and encourage the children to use these skills at the show. Provide a few captions to help explain the process behind each art project. If the group was held within a therapeutic setting, make sure that you have obtained written informed consent from all parents before displaying the children's artwork.

Appendix B

Give it to Me Straight: Summary of the Book for Busy Parents

Art as an Early Intervention Tool for Children with Autism is designed to provide you with information and advice on how to design therapeutic art activities for young children on the spectrum. You will also find the book helpful for people with ASD of any age who are just beginning to develop their foundational drawing skills, or if you and your child are making the transition from using art in a purely recreational sense to using art to tackle developmental, cognitive, or emotional goals. After one or two evenings of reading, I hope your increased knowledge of art materials and ability to empathize with the child will make it much easier for you to wrap your head around how to design productive, individualized activities for (and with) your child.

Chapter 1 is about *who* the techniques in this book are designed for and briefly describes their needs. The explanation of autism and the spectrum of its symptoms will be useful for students and artists. (Seasoned therapists, educators, and parents may want to skim the information.) Of the three major deficit areas of autism, I argue that well-designed art projects are the best approach for tackling the least-often addressed deficit: imagination skills. More information on autism can be found at the reputable websites listed at the end of the book.

Chapter 2 is about *why* this work is important. It describes the basic argument for the inclusion of therapeutic art activities in the early intervention programming of children with ASD. It provides condensed, understandable information about the developmental progression of early drawing skills as well as tips for helping a child make that first, critical step toward a lifetime of satisfying art experiences—moving past scribbling.

Chapter 3 is about *what* you will see when making art with a child with ASD. A unique feature of this book, artwork characteristics that seem to be related to ASD symptoms, are described and organized in Chapter 3. These characteristics could be seen in any child's artwork, but it is their pervasive and common presence in the work of children with ASD that makes them noteworthy. Keep in mind that these are characteristics to work around and work with, but rarely if ever to work directly against. Special consideration of therapeutic intervention with children who have artistic savant skills is provided at the end.

Chapters 4, 5, and 6 are about *how* to work with your child or student. They provide advice on major treatment goals to tackle (Chapter 4), art materials to use (Chapter 5), and how to make adaptations (Chapter 6). The projects and advice are expanded a bit to include older children, so that you will have a sense of what you and your child are working toward.

Remember, the information (especially information about projects) is selective and not all-inclusive; if you find yourself thinking of goals and projects not listed, then you are beginning to synthesize the information and the book has been successful. The best projects are the ones designed with a specific child in mind.

When the child has acquired foundational skills, then art can be a great motivator and organizer when working on early socialization skills. In Appendix A, you will find a list of art projects designed specifically for a group setting. If when you have finished the book you want to continue your studies, the references and recommended reading list will provide you with a comprehensive list of resources on art and autism, all of which had an influence on the development of this book.

If you are reading this with a specific child in mind, then I encourage you to try out a project or two, especially if you do not consider yourself to be "artistic." The information will help you get organized, so all you have to do is relax and be open to a potentially very enriching experience with your child or student. The rewards of seeing your child experience the relief of successful self-expression and acquire skills that will help in school will be well worth it.

References

American Psychiatric Association (2000) *Diagnostic and Statistical Manual of Mental Disorders* (4th edn., text revision). Washington, DC: American Psychiatric Association.

Baron-Cohen, S. and Bolton, P. (1993) *Autism: The Facts.* Oxford: Oxford University Press.

Bartlett, J. (1992) *Bartlett's Familiar Quotations* (J. Kaplan, ed.). Boston, MA: Little, Brown, & Co., p.613.

Bettelheim, B. (1967) *The Empty Fortress: Infantile Autism and the Birth of the Self.* New York, NY: Free Press.

Centers for Disease Control and Prevention (2007, February 8) 'CDC releases new data on autism spectrum disorders (ASDs) from multiple communities in the United States.' Available at www.cdc.gov/media/pressrel/2007/r070208.htm, accessed on December 17, 2008.

Charman, T. and Baron-Cohen, S. (1993) 'Drawing development in autism: The intellectual to visual realism shift.' *British Journal of Developmental Psychology 11,* 171–185.

Craig, J., Baron-Cohen, S., and Scott, F. (2001) 'Drawing ability in autism: A window into the imagination.' *Israel Journal of Psychiatry 38,* 242–253.

Dissanayake, E. (1995) *Homo Aestheticus: Where Art Comes from and Why.* Seattle, WA: University of Washington Press.

Edwards, B. (1999) *The New Drawing on the Right Side of the Brain.* New York, NY: Putnam.

Evans, K. and Dubowski, J. (2001) *Art Therapy with Children on the Autistic Spectrum: Beyond Words.* London: Jessica Kingsley Publishers.

Gray, C. (1994) *Comic Strip Conversations.* Arlington, TX: Future Horizons.

Gray, C. and White, A. L. (1992) *My Social Stories Book.* London: Jessica Kingsley Publishers.

Henley, D. (1989) 'Nadia revisited: A study into the nature of regression in the autistic savant syndrome.' *Art Therapy: Journal of the American Art Therapy Association 6,* 43–56.

Henley, D. (1992) *Exceptional Children, Exceptional Art: Teaching Art to Special Needs.* Worcester, MA: Davis Publications.

Henley, D. (2002) *Clayworks in Art Therapy.* London: Jessica Kingsley Publishers.

Kellogg, R. (1969) *Analyzing Children's Art.* Palo Alto, CA: National Press Books.

Lowenfeld, V. (1947) *Creative and Mental Growth: A Textbook on Art Education.* New York, NJ: Macmillan.

Lowenfeld, V. (1952) *Creative and Mental Growth* (revised edn.). New york, NJ: Macmillan.

Lowenfeld, V. (1957) *Creative and Mental Growth* (3rd edn.). New York, NJ: Macmillan.

Lowenfeld, V. and Brittain, W. L. (1964) *Creative and Mental Growth* (4th edn.). New York, NJ: Macmillan.

Lowenfeld, V. and Brittain, W. L. (1970) *Creative and Mental Growth* (5th edn.). New York, NJ: Macmillan.

Lowenfeld, V. and Brittain, W. L. (1975) *Creative and Mental Growth* (6th edn.). New York, NJ: Macmillan.

Lowenfeld, V. and Brittain, W. L. (1982) *Creative and Mental Growth* (7th edn.). New York, NJ: Macmillan.

Lowenfeld, V. and Brittain, W. L. (1987) *Creative and Mental Growth* (8th edn.). Upper Saddle River, NJ: Prentice Hall.

Lusebrink, V. B. (1990) *Imagery and Visual Expression in Therapy.* New York: Plenum Press.

Martin, N. (2005) *Look at Me: Assessing Portrait Drawings Made by Children with Autism.* Unpublished Master's thesis, School of the Art Institute of Chicago.

Martin, N. (2008) 'Assessing portrait drawings created by children and adolescents with autism spectrum disorder.' *Art Therapy: Journal of the American Art Therapy Association 25,* 1, 15–23.

Mukhopadhyay, T. R. (2008) *How Can I Talk if My Lips Don't Move?: Inside My Autistic Mind.* New York, NY: Arcade Publishing, p.152.

Rimland, B. (1978) 'Savant Capabilities of Autistic Children and their Cognitive Implications.' In G. Serban (ed.) *Cognitive Defects in the Development of Mental Illness.* New York, NY: Brunner/Mazel.

Rossol, M. (1994) *The Artist's Complete Health and Safety Guide* (2nd edn.). New York, NY: Allworth Press.

Sacks, O. (1996) *An Anthropologist on Mars: Seven Paradoxical Tales.* New York, NY: Vintage Books, p.259.

Selfe, L. (1983) *Normal and Anomalous Representational Drawing Ability in Children.* London: Academic Press.

Treffert, D. (1989) *Extraordinary People: Understanding Savant Syndrome.* New York, NY: Ballantine Books.

Webster's New World Dictionary of the American Language (1962) (college edn.). Cleveland, OH: World.

White, L. M. (2002) *Printmaking as Therapy.* London: Jessica Kingsley Publishers.

Willoughby, S. J. (2003) *Art of the M.I.N.D.: The Art Collection of the UC Davis M.I.N.D. Institute.* Sacramento, CA: Regents of the University of California.

World Health Organization (1992) *International Classification of Diseases* (10th edn. text revision). Geneva: WHO.

Recommended resources

This section provides additional references from the fields of art, art therapy, art education, ASD, psychology, and social services that are relevant to the topic of art and autism. Books, research articles, and websites are included. All of these references had an influence on the development of this book. A regularly updated list can be found on my website at www.arttherapyandautism.com. Feel free to contact me if I am missing a reference that should be included. Unless otherwise stated all websites were accessed in December 2008.

Art therapy

*Aach-Feldman, S. and Kunkle-Miller, C. (2001) 'Developmental Art Therapy.' In J. A. Rubin (ed.) *Approaches to Art Therapy: Theory and Technique* (2nd edn.). Philadelphia, PA: Brunner-Routledge.

*Anderson, F. (1992) *Art for All the Children: Approaches to Art Therapy for Children with Disabilities.* Springfield, IL: Charles C. Thomas.

*Banks, S., Davis, P., Howard, V., and McLaughlin, T. (1993) 'The effects of directed art activities on the behavior of young children with disabilities: A multi-element baseline analysis.' *Art Therapy: Journal of the American Art Therapy Association 10*, 4, 235–240.

Bentivegna, S., Schwartz, L., and Deschner, D. (1983) 'Case study: The use of art with an autistic child in residential care.' *American Journal of Art Therapy 22*, 51–56.

Betts, D. J. (2001) 'Special report: The art of art therapy: Drawing individuals out in creative ways.' *The Advocate: Magazine of the Autism Society of America 34*, 3, 22–23 (29).

Betts, D. J. (2003) 'Developing a projective drawing test: Experiences with the Face Stimulus Assessment (FSA).' *Art Therapy: Journal of the American Art Therapy Association 20*, 2, 7–82.

Emery, M. J. (2004) 'Art therapy as an intervention for autism.' *Art Therapy: Journal of the American Art Therapy Association 21*, 143–147.

Fox, L. (1998) 'Lost in Space: The Relevance of Art Therapy with Clients who have Autism or Autistic Features.' In M. Rees (ed.) *Drawing on Difference: Art Therapy with People who have Learning Difficulties.* New York, NY: Routledge.

Gabriels, R. (2003) 'Art Therapy with Children who have Autism and Their Families.' In C. Malchiodi (ed.) *Handbook of Art Therapy*. New York, NY: Guilford Press.

Henley, D. (1989) 'Artistic Giftedness in the Multiply Handicapped.' In H. Wadeson, J. Durkin, and D. Perach (eds) *Advances in Art Therapy*. New York, NY: John Wiley & Sons.

Henley, D. (1992) 'Therapeutic and aesthetic application of video with the developmentally disabled.' *The Arts in Psychotherapy 18*, 441–447.

Henley, D. (2000) 'Blessings in disguise: Idiomatic expression as a stimulus in group art therapy with children.' *Art Therapy: Journal of the American Art Therapy Association 17*, 4, 270–275.

Henley, D. (2001) 'Annihilation anxiety and fantasy in the art of children with Asperger's Syndrome and others on the autistic spectrum.' *American Journal of Art Therapy 39*, 113–121.

*Kiendi, C., Hooyenga, K., and Trenn, E. (1997) 'Empowered to scribble.' *Art Therapy: Journal of the American Art Therapy Association 14*, 37–43.

Kornreich, T. Z. and Schimmel, B. F. (1991) 'The world is attacked by great big snowflakes: Art therapy with an autistic boy.' *American Journal of Art Therapy 29*, 7–84.

Noble, J. (2001) 'Art as an Instrument for Creating Social Reciprocity: Social Skills Group for Children with Autism.' In S. Riley (ed.) *Group Process Made Visible: Group Art Therapy*. Philadelphia, PA: Brunner-Routledge.

*Pounsett, H., Parker, K., Hawtin, A. and Collins, S. (2006) 'Examination of the changes that take place during an art therapy intervention.' *Inscape: International Journal of Art Therapy 11*, 2, 79–101.

*Riley, S. (2004) 'Multi-Family Group Art Therapy: Treating Families with a Disabled Family Member.' In S. Riley (ed.) *Integrative Approaches to Family Art Therapy* (2nd edn.). Chicago, IL: Magnolia Street.

*Roth, E. (2001) 'Behavioral Art Therapy.' In J. A. Rubin (ed.) *Approaches to Art Therapy: Theory and Technique* (2nd edn) Philadelphia, PA: Brunner-Routledge.

Scanlon, K. (1993) 'Art therapy with autistic children.' *Pratt Institute Creative Arts Therapy Review, 14*, 34–43.

Silver, R. A. (1989) *Developing Cognitive and Creative Skills through Art: Programs for Children with Communication Disorders or Learning Disabilities* (3rd edn. revised). New York, NY: Albin Press.

*Silver, R. (2001) 'Assessing and Developing Cognitive Skills through Art.' In J. A. Rubin (ed.) *Approaches to Art Therapy: Theory and Technique* (2nd edn.). Philadelphia, PA: Brunner-Routledge.

Stack, M. (1998) 'Humpty Dumpty's Shell: Working with Autistic Defence Mechanisms in Art Therapy.' In M. Rees (ed.) *Drawing on Difference: Art Therapy with People who have Learning Difficulties*. New York, NY: Routledge.

Does not discuss autism, but contains useful information or techniques.

Art, Art education, and Arts advocacy

*Anderson, F. (1978) *Art for All the Children: A Creative Sourcebook for the Impaired Child.* Springfield, IL: Charles C. Thomas.

Arts Access Australia: www.artsaccessaustralia.org

Davalos, S. (1999) *Making Sense of Art: Sensory-Based Art Activities for Children with Autism, Asperger's Syndrome and other Pervasive Developmental Disorders.* Shawnee Mission, KS: Autism Asperger Publishing Co.

Flowers, T. (1992) *Reaching the Child with Autism through Art.* Arlington, TX: Future Horizons.

Kellman, J. (2001) *Autism, Art, and Children: The Stories We Draw.* Westport, CT: Bergin & Garvey.

Lancelle, M. and Lesada, J. (2006) *Sundays with Matthew: A Young Boy with Autism and an Artist Share their Sketchbooks.* Shawnee Mission, KS: Autism Asperger Publishing Co.

National Arts and Disability Center: http://nadc.ucla.edu/ (They have a satellite program at UCLA's Tarjan Center: http://tarjancenter.ucla.edu/whatwedo.cfm)

*Pemberton, E. and Nelson, K. (1987) 'Using interactive graphic challenges to foster young children's drawing ability.' *Visual Arts Research 13*, 2, 29–41.

Very Special Arts: www.vsarts.org

Artist savants

Bayliss, S. (2004, October) 'Showcasing "neurodiversity": Artists with autism, cerebral palsy, and other disabilities are attracting mainstream attention.' *ARTnews*, 103, 778.

Hall, E. (2004, March 4) 'All kinds of ants: What Gregory Blackstock's autism has to do with his art.' *The Stranger.* Available at www.thestranger.com/seattle/Content?oid=17340, accessed on 21 December 2008.

Karlins, N. F. (2004) 'Is autistic artistic?' *artnet.* Available at www.artnet.com/magazine/features/karlins/karlins1-21-05.asp, accessed on 21 December 2008.

Rexer, L. (2002) *Jonathan Lerman: Drawings by an Artist with Autism.* New York, NY: George Braziller.

Daniel Muller's website: www.geocities.com/dansweb2000

Jessica Park's website: www.jessicapark.com

Mark Rimland's website: www.markrimland.com

Richard Wawro's website: www.wawro.net

Donna Williams' website: www.donnawilliams.net

Stephen Wiltshire's website: www.stephenwiltshire.co.uk

The Wisconsin Medical Society (a center fueled by the scholarly work on savants by Darold Treffert) has a wonderful collection of online videos of people with art savant skills. A must see. www.wisconsinmedicalsociety.org

Does not discuss autism, but contains useful information or techniques.

http://en.wikipedia.org/wiki/Autistic_artist

http://www.neurodiversity.com/art_poetry.html

Autism families

Family members of people with autism using art to cope, share their experiences, and process feelings.

Collier, V. (2005) 'A portrait of autism: A mother's interpretation revealed.' *The Advocate: Magazine of the Autism Society of America 38*, 1, 22–25.

www.genrecookshop.com

Autism Spectrum Disorder

For a much more complete and scientific definition of ASDs than my own, please visit any or all of these reputable websites, which were all accessed in December 2008. They will point you toward a wealth of printed materials.

Autism Research Institute, Defeat Autism Now (DAN): www.autism.com

Autism Society of America: www.autism-society.org

Autism Speaks (recently merged with Cure Autism Now) and the Autism Genetic Resource Exchange (AGRE): www.autismspeaks.org

Centers for Disease Control and Prevention: www.cdc.gov

National Institute of Mental Health: www.nimh.nih.gov

www.autism-resources.com (An incredible warehouse of autism information. Don't miss the bibliography section under "Autism FAQ.")

www.autismtoday.com (Resources and information on autism.)

www.firstsigns.org (A non-profit organization dedicated to early detection and intervention.)

www.neurodiversity.com (Links to a variety of related websites. Don't miss www.neurodiversity.com/art_music.html for art, music, and drama therapy references.)

Watch for research coming out of these universities:
University of California (Davis, Los Angeles, Santa Barbara, San Diego)
University of Cambridge, UK
University of Kansas (Lawrence)
University of North Carolina (Chapel Hill)
Yale University
University of Pittsburgh
University of Washington

www.autismarts.com (Great resource on artists and information from around the world.)

Galleries and collections

The University of California at Davis MIND Institute art collection online: http://www. ucdmc.ucdavis.edu/news/images/mind/artists.html

The Vanderbilt Kennedy Center at Vanderbilt University (Nashville, TN) showcases artwork by and about people with disabilities: http://vanderbilt.edu/site/services/disabilityser-vices/artsanddisabilities.aspx

Psychology, counseling, special education, and social work

Charman, T. and Baron-Cohen, S. (1992) 'Understanding drawings and beliefs: A further test of the metarepresentation theory of autism.' *Journal of Child Psychology and Psychiatry 33*, 6, 1105–1112.

Cox, M. (1999) 'Contrasting styles of drawing in gifted individuals with autism.' *Autism 3*, 4, 39–409.

Epp, K. (2008) 'Outcome-based evaluation of a social skills program using art therapy and group therapy for children on the autism spectrum.' *Children & Schools 30*, 1, 2–36.

Osborne, J. (2003) 'Art and the child with autism: Therapy or education?' *Early Child Development and Care 173*, 411–423.

Pring, L. and Hermelin, B. (1993) 'Bottle, tulip and wineglass: Semantic and structural picture processing by savant artists.' *Journal of Child Psychology and Psychiatry 34*, 8, 1365–1385.

Pring, L., Hermelin, B., and Heavey, L. (1995) 'Savants, segments, art and autism.' *Journal of Child Psychology and Psychiatry 36*, 6, 1065–1076.

Studios and artist workshops

These are community art studios designed especially to accommodate talented artists with neurodevelopmental disabilities. They are usually staffed by artists, art teachers, art thera-pists (those who prefer to work in non-clinical settings), volunteers, and students. These studios foster recreational pleasure, art skill development, relational skills, and sometimes even employment (through artwork sales) and are exceptionally cool places to visit and sup-port (and are often not-for-profit organizations). More can be found at: http://nadc.ucla.edu/ VaCenters.cfm or http://nadc.ucla.edu/resources.cfm.

www.accessiblearts.org (Kansas City, KS)

www.art-enables.org (Washington, DC)

www.littlecityarts.org/ (Palatine, IL)

www.artsoflife.org (Chicago, IL)

www.artsproject.org.au (Northcote, Victoria, Australia)

www.artsunbound.org (Orange, NJ)

www.carousel.org.uk (Brighton, United Kingdom)

www.creativityexplored.org (San Francisco, CA)

http://creativegrowth.org (Oakland, CA)

http://gatewayarts.org (Brookline, MA)

www.kcat.ie (Ireland)

http://magicpaintbrushproject.org (Johnson City/Binghamton, NY)
www.outsidethelinesstudio.org (Medford, MA)

www.passionworks.org (Athens, OH)

www.projectonward.org (Chicago, IL)

www.studiobythetracks.org (Irondale, AL)

www.spindleworks.org (Brunswick, ME)

More useful websites

Accessed on 20 December 2008.

American Red Cross *www.redcross.org*

American Sign Language (ASL) *www.handspeak.com*

Americans with Disabilities Act (ADA) *www.ada.gov*

Autism family support groups *www.autism-society.org*

www.autismspeaks.org

Boardmaker® software *www.mayer-johnson.com*

Individuals with Disabilities Education Act (IDEA) *http://idea.ed.gov*

Picture Exchange Communication System (PECS) *www.pecs.com*

Resources on adaptive tools *www.adaptivechild.com*

Index